ULTIMATE ROCK RIFFS

100 HEART-STOPPING MOMENTS FROM THE GREATEST SONGS OF ROCK

Publisher and Creative Director: Nick Wells
Project Editor and Picture Research: Sara Robson
Art Director and Layout Design: Mike Spender
Digital Design and Production: Chris Herbert

Special thanks to: Laura Bulbeck, Helen Crust, Stephen Feather, Anna Groves, Amanda Leigh, Geoffrey Meadon and Polly Prior

First published 2013 by
FLAME TREE PUBLISHING
Crabtree Hall, Crabtree Lane
Fulham, London SW6 6TY
United Kingdom

www.flametreepublishing.com

Music information site: www.flametreemusic.com

13 15 17 16 14

1 3 5 7 9 10 8 6 4 2

The CIP record for this book is available from the British Library.

ISBN: 978-0-85775-395-3

Printed in Singapore

ULTIMATE ROCK RIFFS

100 HEART-STOPPING MOMENTS FROM THE GREATEST SONGS OF ROCK

JOEL McIVER

FOREWORD BY ROBB FLYNN (MACHINE HEAD)

FLAME TREE PUBLISHING

CONTENTS

HOW TO USE THIS BOOK

ULTIMATE ROCK RIFFS is designed to be easy to navigate. The 100 entries are organized alphabetically by each band or artist's name. When more than one song is included per band or artist, these are further organized according to each song's earliest release date (either in the UK or US).

Beneath the band or artist's name and the song title for each entry, you will find information about the song, the riff and the context in which it was created. You'll also find out about the song's genres, when and where it was recorded, who produced it and who the band members were.

At the end of each entry you'll find a short web link to a **YouTube** video of the song – usually either a live performance or the original music video. Simply type this into your web browser or search engine and rediscover the riff for yourself. **And** if that isn't enough, you'll also find a **QR code** link. Scan this using any **free QR code reader app** on your **smartphone** (e.g. iPhone or Android) and it'll take you straight to the video.

short web link for the video

QR code for the video

PUBLISHER'S NOTE

When we started thinking about who and what should be included in this book, the first thing we had to consider was, what exactly do we mean by a 'rock riff'? The second was, what qualifies it as 'ultimate'? So, before we go into the details about what's in and what's not, let's try to answer these questions.

WHAT IS A ROCK RIFF?

Without getting too technical, a riff is a short, memorable musical phrase, which is often repeated over changing melodies. The term itself is most closely associated with rock and jazz music. Having clarified that point, what we are really talking about here goes beyond the simple riff – this book is more about 'riff-driven' songs, in particular. These are the songs that rely on a repeated instrumental riff as the basis of their most prominent melodies. The riff is often used to anchor the song in the ears of the listener. And that's the beauty about this type of song – you don't have to be musically gifted to spot one. Perhaps that's the reason they've proved to be so popular with songwriters over the past 60 years, or so.

Now, as for what we mean by 'rock' music, well that's another matter. Essentially, 'rock' music is the genre that emerged in the 1950s from the coming together of various roots musics – an exhilarating blend of early rock'n'roll, rhythm and blues and country.

Since those early days, it has become the soundtrack of youth, with each subsequent generation taking it, shaping it and making it their own. The result is a genre as diverse as it is exciting, often with elements of blues, pop, soul, funk and country thrown in for good measure. So, for the purposes of this book, we're not just talking about the standard four-piece band with a lead singer, a couple of guitarists and a drummer, although they are well represented here. Instead we're focusing on the best riff-driven songs in the history of popular music, with songwriters coming in from every side of the rock spectrum and from every decade since the 1950s.

WHAT QUALIFIES AS ULTIMATE?

In our opinion, the 'ultimate' rock riffs are the ones that you recognize from the first chord, or at least the first bar – they have immediate impact and always bring a smile to the face, they are the identity and the backbone of a song, whether created on guitar, keyboard or drums. Everyone has their opinions on the best-ever riffs, and there will never be a consensus – but we've had a go! We've also had a go at listing the top riffing guitarists (*see* below). Without these guys, this book wouldn't be the same.

TOP RIFFING GUITARISTS

1. Jimmy Page (Led Zeppelin)
2. Ritchie Blackmore (Deep Purple)
3. Keith Richards (The Rolling Stones)
4. Slash (Guns N' Roses)
5. Angus Young (AC/DC)
6. Jimi Hendrix (The Jimi Hendrix Experience)
7. Tony Iommi (Black Sabbath)
8. John Lennon (The Beatles)
9. Eddie Van Halen (Van Halen)
10. Kurt Cobain (Nirvana)
11. Dave Davies (The Kinks)
12. Eric Clapton (Cream)
13. Chuck Berry (solo)
14. James Hetfield (Metallica)
15. Randy Rhoads (Ozzy Osbourne)
16. 'Dimebag' Darrell Abbott (Pantera)
17. Mark Knopfler (Dire Straits)
18. Joe Perry (Aerosmith)
19. Pete Townshend (The Who)
20. Tom Morello (Rage Against The Machine)

OUR ULTIMATE SELECTION

We knew when we started thinking about the song selection that this was never going to be an easy process, and boy were we right about that! Nothing divides opinion and causes more arguments around here than our musical tastes. Let's just say there were a few editorial meetings that won't be forgotten in a hurry. We won't go through the ins and outs of why each song was chosen – frankly, we don't have the space. Instead, we'll leave you to be the judge on whether you agree with our decisions.

And, as if agreeing a list of 100 songs to be included wasn't enough, we've taken things a step further and categorized our selection into a 1–100 listing in a bid to come up with what is the best riff-driven rock song of all time. It should be noted that this list (*see* pages 12–13), is purely **subjective** and is intended to provoke a lively and impassioned debate about whether Deep Purple's 'Smoke On The Water' really should take the crown, or perhaps it seems obvious to you that it should be Led Zeppelin's 'Whole Lotta Love'. To add even more fuel to the fire, we asked our Foreword writer, the esteemed Robb Flynn of Machine Head, to come up with his list of best-ever riffs (*see* pages 18–19). If you'd like to give us your version of the top 100 riffs, tell us about a song you think we've missed, or if you just generally want to agree with what you've read then get in touch. Whatever your opinion, we'd love to hear it. You can reach us in all the usual ways: on **twitter** (@FlameTreeMusic), on **facebook** (flametreepublishing), through our **website** (flametreepublishing.com) or by **email** (riffs@flametreemusic.com).

OUR ULTIMATE TOP 100 ROCK RIFFS

1. 'Smoke On The Water' (Deep Purple)
2. 'Sweet Child O' Mine' (Guns N' Roses)
3. 'Smells Like Teen Spirit' (Nirvana)
4. 'Back In Black' (AC/DC)
5. '(I Can't Get No) Satisfaction' (The Rolling Stones)
6. 'Whole Lotta Love' (Led Zeppelin)
7. 'Sunshine Of Your Love' (Cream)
8. 'You Really Got Me' (The Kinks)
9. 'Purple Haze' (The Jimi Hendrix Experience)
10. 'Voodoo Child (Slight Return)' (The Jimi Hendrix Experience)
11. 'Johnny B Goode' (Chuck Berry)
12. 'Paranoid' (Black Sabbath)
13. 'Enter Sandman' (Metallica)
14. 'Layla' (Derek & The Dominos)
15. 'Walk This Way' (Aerosmith)
16. 'Day Tripper' (The Beatles)
17. 'Foxy Lady' (The Jimi Hendrix Experience)
18. 'Iron Man' (Black Sabbath)
19. 'Heartbreaker' (Led Zeppelin)
20. 'Crazy Train' (Ozzy Osbourne)
21. 'Black Dog' (Led Zeppelin)
22. 'Money For Nothing' (Dire Straits)
23. 'Oh, Pretty Woman' (Roy Orbison)
24. 'Welcome To The Jungle' (Guns N' Roses)
25. 'Walk' (Pantera)
26. 'Ain't Talkin' 'Bout Love' (Van Halen)
27. 'In-A-Gadda-Da-Vida' (Iron Butterfly)
28. 'Ace Of Spades' (Motörhead)
29. 'Paradise City' (Guns N' Roses)
30. 'Eye Of The Tiger' (Survivor)
31. 'Sweet Home Alabama' (Lynyrd Skynyrd)
32. 'Frankenstein' (The Edgar Winter Group)
33. 'Bad To The Bone' (George Thorogood & The Destroyers)
34. 'Brown Sugar' (The Rolling Stones)
35. 'Under The Bridge' (Red Hot Chili Peppers)
36. 'Summertime Blues' (Eddie Cochran)
37. 'Jumpin' Jack Flash' (The Rolling Stones)
38. 'American Woman' (The Guess Who)
39. 'Wild Thing' (The Troggs)
40. 'Rebel Rebel' (David Bowie)
41. 'Roadhouse Blues' (The Doors)
42. 'Breaking The Law' (Judas Priest)
43. 'Runnin' With The Devil' (Van Halen)
44. 'Highway To Hell' (AC/DC)
45. 'Electric Eye' (Judas Priest)
46. 'Outshined' (Soundgarden)
47. 'Hells Bells' (AC/DC)
48. 'Gimme All Your Lovin'' (ZZ Top)

49. 'Master Of Puppets' (Metallica)
50. 'Kashmir' (Led Zeppelin)
51. 'Raining Blood' (Slayer)
52. 'Panama' (Van Halen)
53. 'Start Me Up' (The Rolling Stones)
54. 'N.I.B.' (Black Sabbath)
55. 'Pinball Wizard' (The Who)
56. 'Stranglehold' (Ted Nugent)
57. 'Wipe Out' (The Surfaris)
58. '(Don't Fear) The Reaper' (Blue Öyster Cult)
59. 'All Day And All Of The Night' (The Kinks)
60. 'Up Around The Bend' (Creedence Clearwater Revival)
61. 'Life In The Fast Lane' (The Eagles)
62. 'A New Level' (Pantera)
63. 'All Right Now' (Free)
64. 'Are You Gonna Go My Way' (Lenny Kravitz)
65. 'I Feel Fine' (The Beatles)
66. 'The Boys Are Back In Town' (Thin Lizzy)
67. 'Paperback Writer' (The Beatles)
68. 'The Trooper' (Iron Maiden)
69. 'The Spirit Of Radio' (Rush)
70. 'Hysteria' (Muse)
71. 'Symphony Of Destruction' (Megadeth)
72. 'Seven Nation Army' (The White Stripes)
73. 'Wake Up' (Rage Against The Machine)
74. 'Davidian' (Machine Head)
75. 'Run To The Hills' (Iron Maiden)
76. 'Born To Be Wild' (Steppenwolf)
77. 'Song 2' (Blur)
78. 'Plug In Baby' (Muse)
79. 'Beat It' (Michael Jackson)
80. 'Killing In The Name' (Rage Against The Machine)
81. 'Hey Hey, My My (Into The Black)' (Neil Young & Crazy Horse)
82. 'I Wanna Be Your Dog' (The Stooges)
83. 'Have Love, Will Travel' (The Sonics)
84. 'Dr Feelgood' (Mötley Crüe)
85. 'Tie Your Mother Down' (Queen)
86. 'Motorcycle Emptiness' (Manic Street Preachers)
87. 'Sunday Bloody Sunday' (U2)
88. 'I'm Free' (The Who)
89. 'Slither' (Velvet Revolver)
90. 'No One Knows' (Queens Of The Stone Age)
91. 'Mr Brightside' (The Killers)
92. 'Beast And The Harlot' (Avenged Sevenfold)
93. 'Mind Eraser, No Chaser' (Them Crooked Vultures)
94. 'Take Me Out' (Franz Ferdinand)
95. 'Cochise' (Audioslave)
96. 'Hunting For Witches' (Bloc Party)
97. 'I Believe In A Thing Called Love' (The Darkness)
98. 'In The Morning' (Razorlight)
99. 'American Idiot' (Green Day)
100. 'Lego House' (Ed Sheeran)

FOREWORD: ROBB FLYNN

The first riff that I ever played air guitar to was Van Halen's cover of The Kinks' 'You Really Got Me'. My friend Lisa Sgroe and I cut cardboard guitars out of her mom's new refrigerator box, took a felt pen, drew strings and tuning pegs, and then stood in front of the mirror rocking the hell out. There was something so heavy about that riff, with its tone so heavy and jagged, that drove this then-fourth-grader bananas.

That is the power of a riff – that it can actually move you, make you shake, make you feel an emotion, make you want to jump, and thrash, and headbang, and boogie, and scream, and cry, and in some cases, even get horny. Don't believe me? Put on Led Zeppelin's 'The Lemon Song' from *Led Zeppelin II*: it's a sex act made into music! It was also the first riff I ever learned how to play on guitar. I wasn't even really into Zeppelin at that point in my life: that appreciation would come much later, but I had heard that song a million times on my local radio station KOME in San Jose, California – and one day, while I was playing my nylon-string acoustic (which was missing two strings), I stumbled onto that riff. I may not have loved Zeppelin at that point, but man, I loved playing that riff.

A few days later I bragged to a friend of mine, a weed dealer named Roger, that I could play Led Zeppelin. He turned to me and said 'Yeah, but can you do a power chord?' I was curious and asked him what that was. His answer was perfect stoner wisdom: 'It's exactly like it sounds: it's the sound of power.' He taught me how to play 'Sweet Leaf' by Black Sabbath – a band I would worship for the rest of my life – and on that day, stoned out of my mind, learning power chords and riffs, my life literally changed direction. That week I quit jiu-jitsu, started playing guitar non-stop, and was officially on the road to heavy metal.

Once your mind discovers this new world, it embarks on a quest for the ultimate riff, the heaviest riff, the simplest crushing riff, the most mind-bogglingly twisted, complex riff, or the most beautiful, elegant riff. They all have their place. Gary Holt of Exodus has written the most riffs that make me want to smash stuff: the riffs on their debut album *Bonded By Blood* are some of the most timeless thrash metal riffs of all time, with songs like 'And Then There Were None', 'A Lesson In Violence' and the savage 'Strike Of The Beast', as well as later Holt riffs like 'Deranged', 'Last Act Of Defiance' and 'Altered Boy'. Such was the impact of Gary Holt on my young life that his solo in 'Bonded By Blood' was the first I ever learned how to play.

Then there's Slayer, whose riffs fill me with anger: my first garage band covered 'Black Magic', and the slow riff in the middle of 'Crypts Of Eternity' is one of the heaviest riffs of all time. Listen to the dark, majestic beauty of 'Seasons In The Abyss' and the vicious, unrelenting, practically incomprehensible heaviness of every single riff in 'Angel Of Death'.

On to Metallica, who wrote the kind of riffs that made me want to take on the world. I remember listening to 'Whiplash' the first time I ever got drunk: I was invincible. The same is true of 'Damage, Inc.' and 'Battery' ... brutal. But Metallica also wrote acoustic riffs which made them stand apart, adding a sad melody to their brand of metal:

the riffs to 'One' and 'Fade To Black' helped define the sound of modern metal. And while I play metal, I love melody, and I love melodic acoustic riffs. Jimi Hendrix's 'Little Wing' is my favourite riff and song of all time. I walked down the aisle to this song when I got married. Such beauty, subtle elegance, and soul, pure heartfelt soul: you can see it and feel it, with its solo that can literally make a grown man cry. I've been trying to master this song for nearly 20 years and I am yet to perfect it.

For those of you who play instruments, that's also the beauty of creating music and of writing riffs. Sometimes writing a riff comes from nowhere: with most of the riffs that I've written which people consider to be 'classic', I couldn't tell you that I felt that way when I wrote them. I'd just think, 'Hmm, pretty cool!' Sometimes they take months to hone (like 'Halo'), sometimes they pour out in a few minutes (like 'Aesthetics Of Hate'), sometimes they hit you when you have the worst flu of your life ('Imperium'), and sometimes they find their way out while you're not even trying. I wrote the chorus for 'Ten Ton Hammer' and most of 'Now I Lay Thee Down' in my head, driving to and from rehearsal. I wrote 'Davidian' on a classical guitar in my then-girlfriend's apartment while hungover one morning.

Riffs are magical in their variety, because they speak to so many areas of your brain. You need the Neanderthal simplicity of AC/DC or Hatebreed to be the yin to the yang of the classical riffage of, say, Yngwie Malmsteen or Rush. There are no rules, there is only the end result – and if that end result makes you feel something, anything, then it's done its job.

Hail The Riff.
Robb Flynn, 2012

ROBB FLYNN'S 100 ULTIMATE RIFFS

AC/DC: 'Back In Black'

AC/DC: 'Highway To Hell'

Aerosmith: 'Dream On'

Aerosmith: 'Walk This Way'

Alice In Chains: 'Dirt'

Anthrax: 'I Am The Law'

Avenged Sevenfold: 'Nightmare'

Beastie Boys: 'Sabotage'

The Beatles: 'Helter Skelter'

The Beatles: 'Sgt Pepper's Lonely Hearts Club Band'

Pat Benatar: 'Heartbreaker'

Biohazard: 'Punishment'

Black Sabbath: 'Iron Man'

Black Sabbath: 'N.I.B.'

Blue Öyster Cult: 'Godzilla'

Bon Jovi: 'You Give Love A Bad Name'

Eric Clapton: 'Cocaine'

The Dead Kennedys: 'Holiday In Cambodia'

Def Leppard: 'Let It Go'

Deftones: 'Diamond Eyes'

Deftones: 'My Own Summer (Shove It)'

Discharge: 'Hell On Earth'

The Eagles: 'Life In The Fast Lane'

Exodus: 'A Lesson In Violence'

Exodus: 'Strike Of The Beast'

Faith No More: 'Surprise! You're Dead!'

Foo Fighters: 'All My Life'

Forbidden: 'Chalice Of Blood'

Foreigner: 'Double Vision'

Green Day: 'American Idiot'

Guns N' Roses: 'It's So Easy'

Guns N' Roses: 'Welcome To The Jungle'

Hatebreed: 'I Will Be Heard'

The Jimi Hendrix Experience: 'Foxy Lady'

The Jimi Hendrix Experience: 'Hey Joe'

Iron Butterfly: 'In-A-Gadda-Da-Vida'

Iron Maiden: 'Prowler'

Iron Maiden: 'The Trooper'

Iron Maiden: 'Wrathchild'

Elton John: 'Saturday Night's All Right For Fighting'

Judas Priest: 'Breaking The Law'

Judas Priest: 'The Green Manalishi (With The Two Pronged Crown)'

Judas Priest: 'Victim Of Changes'

Kansas: 'Carry On Wayward Son'

Korn: 'Blind'

Led Zeppelin: 'Black Dog'

Led Zeppelin: 'Whole Lotta Love'

Lynyrd Skynyrd: 'Saturday Night Special'

Lynyrd Skynyrd: 'Sweet Home Alabama'

Yngwie Malmsteen: 'Anguish And Fear'

Marilyn Manson: 'Beautiful People'

Megadeth: 'Holy Wars ... The Punishment Due'

Megadeth: 'Peace Sells'

Metallica: 'Battery'

Metallica: 'Creeping Death'

Metallica: 'Master Of Puppets'

Steve Miller Band: 'Rock'N Me'

Mötley Crüe: 'Live Wire'

Motörhead: 'Ace Of Spades'

Muse: 'Time Is Running Out'

My Chemical Romance: 'Mama'

Nine Inch Nails: 'Head Like A Hole'

Nirvana: 'Negative Creep'

Nirvana: 'Smells Like Teen Spirit'

Ozzy Osbourne: 'Crazy Train'

Ozzy Osbourne: 'Miracle Man'

Pantera: 'A New Level'

Pantera: 'Walk'

Pearl Jam: 'Evenflow'

Pearl Jam: 'Jeremy'

Tom Petty & The Heartbreakers: 'American Girl'

Pink Floyd: 'Another Brick In The Wall'

Pink Floyd: 'Money'

Poison Idea: 'Alan's On Fire'

The Police: 'Message In A Bottle'

Queen: 'Stone Cold Crazy'

Queens Of The Stone Age: 'You Think I Ain't Worth A Dollar But I Feel Like A Millionaire'

Queensryche: 'The Needle Lies'

Rage Against The Machine: 'Bulls On Parade'

The Rolling Stones: 'Brown Sugar'

The Rolling Stones: 'Honky Tonk Woman'

David Lee Roth: 'Shy Boy'

Run DMC: 'Rock Box'

Rush: 'YYZ'

Scorpions: 'Rock You Like A Hurricane'

Sepultura: 'Roots'

Slayer: 'Angel Of Death'

Slayer: 'Raining Blood'

Slipknot: 'Duality'

Soundgarden: 'Rusty Cage'

Bruce Springsteen: 'Born To Run'

System Of A Down: 'Chop Suey!'

T Rex: '20th Century Boy'

Thin Lizzy: 'Jailbreak'

Tool: 'Sober'

The Troggs: 'Wild Thing'

U2: 'Sunday Bloody Sunday'

Van Halen: 'You Really Got Me'

Vio-Lence: 'Kill On Command'

ZZ Top: 'Cheap Sunglasses'

INTRODUCTION

Welcome to *Ultimate Rock Riffs*, the place to be if your interests include listening to unsociably loud music, annoying your neighbours, or breaking out a trusty guitar – whether made of air or wood.

The 100 songs we've listed in this book represent the very finest riff-based songwriting that the last 60 years of popular music have to offer. Between the editors, publishers and me, this list was pummelled into shape over many long evenings locked in a secret bunker in the Scottish Highlands, with only a case of whisky, the first four Black Sabbath albums, some cheese and biscuits, and a pack of cards for company. The battles raged long into the night, sometimes ending in fisticuffs, as we fought to get our favourites on the list. Should we include more than three songs by Metallica? Do acoustic singer-songwriters like Ed Sheeran deserve to make the cut? Is 'Bad To The Bone' just bad? Does folk music count if you don't like Aran sweaters? Are Jimi Hendrix's versions of Bob Dylan's songs better than the originals? Shouldn't we just make the list 100 Led Zeppelin songs and go to the pub?

All of which begs the question of what a riff is, exactly, and why we should care about it. Musicians know it as an *ostinato*, which sounds like a pasta sauce but actually refers to any repeated pattern of notes that defines a song. However, you don't need musical training to recognize a riff. Whether it's the staccato notes that introduce Deep Purple's 'Smoke On The Water', the smooth chords that begin ZZ Top's 'Gimme All

Your Lovin'', the amazing pattern that underpins 'Beat It' by Michael Jackson, or the pounding progression anchoring 'Walk' by Pantera, most people will react instinctively to a riff when they hear one.

You may be thinking that *Ultimate Rock Riffs* is all about hard rock and heavy metal. Well, it isn't. Riffs do form the basis of many songs from the heavier end of the musical spectrum, and indeed you could do a lot of potential headbanging if you made our 100 songs into a playlist (now there's an idea for a party if we ever heard one), but there's a lot of room for subtlety and emotional expression here, and we've taken full advantage of that. What our 100 songs represent is essentially the best bits of riff-based songwriting ever committed to vinyl, CD or hard drive, whether the composers come from rock, country, folk, blues or soul. There isn't much electronica, hip-hop, funk, jazz or reggae here – although all of those genres are represented at least in passing – because those forms of music focus more on grooves, beats and solos than on repeated riffs. With that in mind, we've been careful to point out when a given song has been transformed by a later cover version into a different form of music, such as Apollo 440's dance version of Van Halen's 'Ain't Talkin' 'Bout Love' or Tina Turner's souled-up cover of The Rolling Stones' '(I Can't Get No) Satisfaction'.

We've also made a point of covering the history of music in a comprehensive fashion. The heyday of the almighty riff was arguably the 1970s, when the holy trinity of Zeppelin, Purple and Sabbath ruled the airwaves before punk came in and made the old rockers look their age, but both before and after that golden era the riffs have come thick and fast. Hendrix, Cream, Iron Butterfly, The Kinks, The Stones and an obscure beat combo called The Beatles were riffing it up way before the 1970s. After that golden decade, songwriters in a multitude of bands have kept the great tradition rolling in bands such as Iron Maiden, Green Day, Guns N' Roses, Judas Priest, Bloc Party, AC/DC, Blur, Dire Straits, The Killers ... we could go on, but we don't want to keep you much longer from reading the entries for yourself.

Your experience of this book may vary depending on your age. If you're under, say, 35, you may be wondering why we didn't include The Offspring or Trivium or Beck. Then again, the over-fifties among you may well already be composing an enraged email to us, calling us morons and demanding to know why Miles Davis, The Grateful Dead or Steely Dan aren't included. In our defence, we can only say that this book is big enough for 100 entries and no more. Now, if we ever get to write a sequel with 1000 riffs in it, we'd really be going places, unless the editorial team ended up killing each other, or (as is more likely) drinking themselves to death before the book even got started. *Ultimate Rock Riffs* can never be more than a teaser, the tippety top of the tip of the iceberg. Use it as a way into music that you may never have heard before, or that you've heard but forgotten about. The great thing about music is that it is infinite and always there. It will always be your friend, your guide, your comfort and your ally. And you can switch it off when you've had enough of it.

We're very fortunate to have the mighty Robb Flynn of Machine Head as our foreword writer. The composer of a stack of monster riffs over his two decades and more as a professional musician, he knows a good riff when he hears one, no matter where it comes from. Actually, that leads me to an important point. Too much riff-based music ends up shovelled by marketing executives towards a particular demographic. Visit any service station and you'll see a parade of tired, grey-faced sales executives

in their late forties perusing the CD racks and buying compilations called *100 Percent Rock Anthems For Father's Day, Volume 12*. These CDs, and believe me we've played them, are compiled by bored catalogue administrators at record companies, and serve no purpose other than to make people think that Motörhead and Lynyrd Skynyrd are for middle-aged dullards. Have they got no souls, we ask. Every song in this book is vibrant, relevant and essential listening for anyone, whether you're a nine-year-old kid discovering rock music for the first time, or a 97-year-old OAP rediscovering the songs from your youth that first made life worth living. Music doesn't need to be allocated a target demographic, and in fact doing so is futile and insulting. Music is bigger than that, hence the free-for-all when it comes to genres and decades that is this book. Enjoy the ride.

Joel McIver, 2012

P.S. I can't help but stick my favourite riff of all time here (skip to the first entry if you don't want to hear any more ramblings from me). It doesn't appear in the main book text because the other staff made me stop writing about it. No, it's not 'I'll Be There For You (Theme From Friends)' by The Rembrandts. It's 'Black Sabbath' by Black Sabbath on the album *Black Sabbath*, an unholy trinity of metal, if you will. The main riff, a tritone in technical terms, is based on the scariest interval ever. In fact, there's a great story attached to it. In the Middle Ages, the tritone (or *diabolus in musica*) is thought to have been banned for religious reasons, until the codification of notation in traditional church music was modified to account for— Shut up (ed.)

ULTI
ROCK

in its infancy in rock music in the late 1970s. Curiously, when the single was released (backed with 'If You Want Blood [You've Got It]'), it only reached No. 47 on the US *Billboard* chart. It was among the last of AC/DC's singles to underperform before the enormous explosion in their popularity that accompanied the death of Scott, the recruitment of Geordie singer Brian Johnson and the epic *Back In Black* album of 1980.

MUSICAL LEGACY

Due to its memorable riffs and anthemic (and still mildly edgy, if you live in Alabama) chorus, 'Highway To Hell' has remained a huge favourite. AC/DC continue to play it live as one of the staple songs in any live set, and its influence has spread into wider cultural awareness through boxers and baseball players using it as their walk-on theme at sporting events. It has been used in cult TV shows like *Family Guy* and *The Simpsons*, and comedic films dealing with diabolical matters or rock music (*Little Nicky*, *School Of Rock*, *Final Destination 2*) have recruited it too. Nowadays 'Highway To Hell' is as much a pub covers band staple as it is a rock classic, and one of AC/DC's all-time classic hits.

GENRES

Hard rock, blues rock, heavy metal

RECORDED

1979 in London

PRODUCER

Robert 'Mutt' Lange

BAND MEMBERS

Bon Scott, Angus Young, Malcolm Young, Cliff Williams, Phil Rudd

ON YOUTUBE  http://flametr.com/highway-to-hell

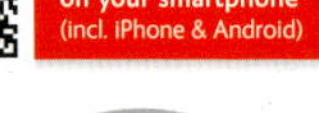

AC/DC

HELLS BELLS

In 1980, Australian hard rockers AC/DC executed a remarkable series of moves in order to survive. Their singer, Bon Scott, died suddenly in February after a mammoth night out in London; the group recruited a new singer, Brian Johnson, in March; and a new album, *Back In Black*, was recorded in May and released in July. Its first song, 'Hells Bells' (note the deliberate omission of an apostrophe, punctuation fans), was a slow, doomy tribute to their fallen comrade, although it didn't specifically refer to his passing. It begins with a bell, tolling slowly, before Angus Young's sinister riff begins, and as such is a perfect introduction to the more upbeat songs that follow. American baseball player Trevor Hoffmann used the song as his entrance music for over a decade. At his retirement ceremony in 2010, Johnson himself appeared to give his congratulations. There was good reason for this, as Hoffmann had helped to keep the song – a subtler, more pensive composition than most of AC/DC's best-known hits – alive for years after its subject was dead and buried.

GENRES

Hard rock, heavy metal

RECORDED

1980 in Nassau, The Bahamas

PRODUCER

Robert 'Mutt' Lange

BAND MEMBERS

Brian Johnson, Angus Young, Malcolm Young, Cliff Williams, Phil Rudd

ON YOUTUBE  http://flametr.com/hells-bells

Scan to see a video on your smartphone (incl. iPhone & Android)

AC/DC

BACK IN BLACK

'Back In Black' is blessed with an opening riff that everyone knows, even people who don't like heavy music or think that the idea of a man in his sixties running around in his school uniform is somewhat unusual. This applies to many of the riffs later in the song, too: it's a veritable cornucopia of catchiness distilled into a rock staple. What's most amazing, after all these years, is that 'Back In Black' and the other songs on the album of the same title were written in such a period of chaos for AC/DC, recovering as they were from the death of singer Bon Scott. That the song has endured so well over the ensuing decades is miraculous, although perhaps its combination of unforgettable riffage, a bombastic theme and that roared chorus line made it destined for long-term glory.

RECORDING AND RELEASE

Perhaps the weather was particularly spectacular in Nassau in the spring of 1980, when AC/DC – with new singer Brian Johnson aboard – convened at Compass Point Studios to record their spectacular comeback album. Angus and Malcolm Young, laying down the riffs with their Gibson SG and Gretsch Jet Firebird respectively, recorded this song with audible swing, pushing against the pulse laid down by Cliff Williams and Phil Rudd and giving the song its essential catchiness. The whole mid-section of the song, a clash of spiraling, duelling guitars, is solid evidence that, whatever else AC/DC were, they were advanced musicians – not a statement often made about this band, whose main strength lies in simple, economical riff patterns. Credit must go to producer Mutt Lange, whose expert grasp of song dynamics was an important factor in giving the song its sheen. The guitars were engineered for maximum control and punch despite their significant gain. Once more, the Youngs showed the world that they possessed

picking hands like few other guitarists. Note that none other than Dave Mustaine of Megadeth, routinely voted one of the world's best guitar players, once stated that Malcolm was one of the top three best rhythm guitar players in the world (he included himself and Metallica's James Hetfield in that elite trio).

MUSICAL LEGACY

Any heavy rock song that soundtracks a reality TV show has by definition transcended its musical boundaries and essentially 'gone viral'. Such was the case with 'Back In Black', which became the theme to a British version of *Big Brother* in the mid-2000s. American comedian Lewis Black used the introduction to the song as his walk-on theme on Comedy Central's *The Daily Show*. Elsewhere, the song has graced animated movie soundtracks such as *Megamind* and more sports fields than could possibly be listed here. Even *The Muppets* have used snatches of 'Back In Black' over the years: how many rock songs can you name that appeal to everyone, from children to superannuated headbangers?

GENRES

Hard rock, heavy metal

RECORDED

1980 in Nassau, The Bahamas

PRODUCER

Robert 'Mutt' Lange

BAND MEMBERS

Brian Johnson, Angus Young, Malcolm Young, Cliff Williams, Phil Rudd

ON YOUTUBE

Scan to see a video on your smartphone (incl. iPhone & Android)

AEROSMITH

WALK THIS WAY

Boston rockers Aerosmith hit gold with their third album, *Toys In The Attic*. On second thoughts, it might be more accurate to say that they hit platinum – eight times! – with it, thanks to immense sales and the public's realization that they were one of America's most convincing mid-1970s groups. The single 'Walk This Way' was one of this much-cherished album's highlights, released in autumn 1975 and becoming a huge hit both domestically and internationally. The riff that begins the song and continues throughout has become one of the staples of any budding rock guitar player's early repertoire, based as it is on a relatively playable sequence of single notes. Steven Tyler's alternately barked and wailed lyrics made the song a perfect candidate for sampling when the hip-hop era got going in earnest a decade later – and in fact this is exactly what happened, when East Coast rap outfit Run DMC re-recorded the song, and made it an even bigger hit the second time around.

RECORDING AND RELEASE

Said to be inspired by a line from the Mel Brooks film *Young Frankenstein*, 'Walk This Way' tells the tale of a young man's rite of passage at a high-school dance. The song's chorus is adapted to involve maximum audience participation at Aerosmith's live shows, although, let's be honest, no one really knows what it means. The Run DMC version makes the most of the drum intro, making it a beefed-up version of Joey Kramer's original two-bar measure with added DJ scratching, and mixes the guitar riff higher in the song for greater impact. For readers in their thirties or younger who first came across the song in this latter version, it's a shock to hear the original Aerosmith cut, to hear how timid the guitar line and drums were. That's a decade of progress in studio technology for you.

Check out the video of the Run DMC song, too; it was at least partly responsible for the return to prominence of the now clean and sober Aerosmith to the public eye in the late 1980s.

MUSICAL LEGACY

It's difficult to overstate the big picture of what happened in guitar music thanks to Run DMC's cover of 'Walk This Way'. The song was the first combination of hip-hop and rock to gain notice on any significant scale, and ushered in a whole new awareness among musicians that the two genres could successfully combine. A 1991 song by Anthrax and Public Enemy called 'Bring The Noise' was equally influential on the emerging rap-rock scene, which rapidly mutated into funk-rock (Faith No More, Living Colour, the Red Hot Chili Peppers), rap-metal (Rage Against The Machine) and ultimately nu-metal (Korn, Limp Bizkit, Slipknot). A raft of rappin', frontin', baseball cap-wearin' rockers came to the fore, although when the wheel of fashion turned once more it wasn't long before most of them returned to wearing denim and leather and denied that they had ever liked rap in the first place.

GENRES

Hard rock

RECORDED

1975 in New York

PRODUCER

Jack Douglas

BAND MEMBERS

Steven Tyler, Joe Perry, Brad Whitford, Tom Hamilton, Joey Kramer

ON YOUTUBE http://flametr.com/walk-this-way

Scan to see a video on your smartphone (incl. iPhone & Android)

AUDIOSLAVE

COCHISE

40

In 2002 rap-metallers Rage Against The Machine had lost their singer (Zack de la Rocha) and grunge icon Chris Cornell had lost his band (Soundgarden). The solution? Form a supergroup, and so Audioslave was born. With the benefit of hindsight, it's clear that Audioslave were a stopgap while the musicians were waiting to re-form Rage Against The Machine and Soundgarden, but at the time the group seemed like a highly exciting new proposition. That said, the riff on which 'Cochise' is founded is hardly new: it's nothing less than an homage to Led Zeppelin, with perhaps a nod towards early 1970s Deep Purple. Morello played it in standard tuning, adding an introduction formed of treated notes through a whammy pedal. The subject was familiar territory for anyone used to Morello's usual inspirations: Cochise was an 18th-century Native American chief who waged war on the invading white man. The result is a mighty song indeed, accompanied by a full bells-and-whistles video in which the band plays against a backdrop of exploding fireworks and much is made of Commerford's painful-looking all-over tattoos. That's rock'n'roll.

GENRES

Alternative metal, heavy metal

RECORDED

2002 in Seattle, Los Angeles and Burbank, California

PRODUCER

Rick Rubin

BAND MEMBERS

Chris Cornell, Tom Morello, Tim Commerford, Brad Wilk

ON YOUTUBE  http://flametr.com/cochise-audio

Scan to see a video on your smartphone (incl. iPhone & Android)

Von Dutch
POWER

AVENGED SEVENFOLD

BEAST AND THE HARLOT

Pitched somewhere between Guns N' Roses-style stadium rock and a slightly tougher but still melodic sound reminiscent of Megadeth, Avenged Sevenfold have consistently drawn huge, and adoring, teenage audiences. While this has drawn sneers from members of the wider heavy metal community, there is no denying the skill of guitarists Zacky Vengeance and Synyster Gates (Zachary Baker and Brian Haner to their mothers), whose shredding and rhythm techniques approach unearthly levels of ability at times. The core riff of this 2006 single involves fast tremolo picking with power chords, and will test the picking hand of any metal guitar student. The solos, primarily executed by Gates, are a splendid combination of wide-interval melodies, sweep picking and divebombs – the essence of modern, melodic playing. Taken from Avenged Sevenfold's third, and probably most successful, album, *City Of Evil*, 'Beast And The Harlot' tells a tale of temptation and lust in Hollywood, with suitably demonic references given the title's Biblical origins. Kids loved it, older metalheads were dismissive, but guitarists everywhere gave the two axemen their approval.

GENRES

Heavy metal

RECORDED

2005 in Houston

PRODUCER

Andrew Murdock

BAND MEMBERS

M. Shadows, Zacky Vengeance, Synyster Gates, Johnny Christ, James 'The Rev' Sullivan

ON YOUTUBE  http://flametr.com/beast-and-the-harlot

Scan to see a video on your smartphone (incl. iPhone & Android)

THE BEATLES

I FEEL FINE

In November 1964, guitar feedback was a thing to be avoided – even if you knew what it was. Amps and PA systems were yet to grow to large enough sizes for feedback to be a common problem. Yet The Beatles used it, deliberately, on the opening note of 'I Feel Fine', no doubt to the horror of the white-coated engineers at the recording studios of the day. This extended note, played on the A string of John Lennon's Gibson semi-acoustic J-160E, resolves after a few seconds into a slinky riff over a nifty descending three-chord pattern, which feeds into the first verse. The fact that Lennon and George Harrison played the riff with such precision says much about their skills as musicians still in their early twenties. A little-known fact about this riff is that it was a high point of a jam between The Beatles and Elvis Presley in Beverly Hills the following year. Apparently the King picked out the 'I Feel Fine' riff on a bass.

GENRES

Rock

RECORDED

1964 in London

PRODUCER

George Martin

BAND MEMBERS

John Lennon, Paul McCartney, George Harrison, Ringo Starr

ON YOUTUBE  http://flametr.com/feel-fine

Scan to see a video on your smartphone (incl. iPhone & Android)

THE BEATLES

DAY TRIPPER

In 1965 the phrase 'prick teaser' was not commonly used in mainstream culture, but The Beatles managed to find a place for this golden term when they wrote 'Day Tripper', a song describing a woman of uncertain moral compass and reliability. Aware that this misogynistic term for a female who refuses to follow up on her initial advances would not be welcomed, The Fab Four told the press and fans that they were actually singing 'big teaser'. Yeah right, John.... However, it was almost impossible to make out the actual words because – wisely – the guitar riff on which 'Day Tripper' was based is both unforgettable in nature and mixed prominently up in the track, allowing the forbidden words to be obscured. John Lennon revealed that he had come up with the riff and the general theme and structure of the song before Paul McCartney finished it off, musically and lyrically, making 'Day Tripper' yet another example of the incredible synergy that existed between these two great songwriting talents.

RECORDING AND RELEASE

'Day Tripper', written in time for release before Christmas 1965, was issued as a double A-side single (remember those?) with the much more sombre 'We Can Work It Out', and became a UK chart-topping hit. The riff itself, a dexterous figure in E ascending to A for a bar before dropping back and then devolving to chords in F♯, has become a staple among Beatles cover bands and, like so many of the band's early riffs, has become practically integrated into rock music's DNA. You'll hear the two guitar tracks from Lennon and Harrison played in near-perfect synch, but with slightly different tones for a wider frequency range. It's interesting to note that at 1'50"

Ludwig
THE

the guitar line vanishes momentarily in a 'drop-out', the result of an error on the studio tape. This error was fixed on compilations such as *1*, released in 2000. Three different videos were shot for the song, directed by Joe McGrath, and can be seen today on YouTube.

MUSICAL LEGACY

In part thanks to the 'prick teaser' story and in part because it's a great song, 'Day Tripper' is one of The Beatles' best-known post-rock'n'roll, pre-psychedelia songs. It has been covered extensively, not just by contemporaries such as Jimi Hendrix but also by later groups such as James Taylor, Whitesnake, Sham 69 and Bad Brains. Not a bad performance for a song which begins and ends with the same, maddeningly catchy, riff. The outro, over which the band repeat 'Day tripper ... day tripper, yeah', seems to go on for ever, slowly fading out. You'll also hear that riff, in company with others by Led Zeppelin and Metallica, bashed out with various degrees of incompetence in guitar shops worldwide, driving the staff insane. Lennon would no doubt be proud.

GENRES

Rock

RECORDED

1965 in London

PRODUCER

George Martin

BAND MEMBERS

John Lennon, Paul McCartney, George Harrison, Ringo Starr

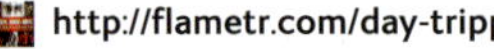

Scan to see a video on your smartphone (Incl. iPhone & Android)

Ludwig
THE

THE BEATLES

PAPERBACK WRITER

By 1966 John Lennon and George Harrison were enjoying a meatier guitar sound than the thinner tones of The Beatles' rock'n'roll years, as evidenced by the warm overdrive of 'Paperback Writer'. Based on smoothly arpeggiated chords and backed by Paul McCartney's flying octave fills on bass, the opening riff pushed forward in the utterly memorable way to which fans had by now become accustomed. Like 'Day Tripper', 'Paperback Writer' is in this book because it is based on that driving *ostinato* and not merely flat-picked or strummed chords. Also like that earlier song, 'Paperback Writer' exits on the same repeated riff and the sung repetition of the title. The inspiration for the lyrics came, according to McCartney in an interview with the late Radio One DJ Jimmy Savile, when an aunt asked him if he could write a song that wasn't about love. Spotting Ringo reading a novel, he duly decided to write about a book instead.

GENRES

Hard rock, power pop

RECORDED

1966 in London

PRODUCER

George Martin

BAND MEMBERS

John Lennon, Paul McCartney, George Harrison, Ringo Starr

ON YOUTUBE  http://flametr.com/paperback-writer

Scan to see a video on your smartphone (incl. iPhone & Android)

CHUCK BERRY

JOHNNY B GOODE

Sure, Elvis Presley and Carl Perkins had spent a couple of years inventing rock'n'roll before Chuck Berry emerged in April 1958 with 'Johnny B Goode', but if there's a better candidate for the first rock'n'roll guitar riff, we'd like to hear it. That opening riff, which recurs at regular points through the song, is punctuated by bass and drums in such a way that it draws the attention of anyone who hears it. It's probably Chuck's signature song, despite the popularity of 'Maybellene' and his other hits. There's no mistaking the song or indeed its singer, who is by all accounts a rather curious but talented cove whose exploits with hidden cameras and what have you (no details, no lawsuits, m'lud) have made him as notorious for his personal life as for his music.

RECORDING AND RELEASE

You've heard dozens of versions of 'Johnny B Goode' in your life, some faithful to the original, some radically different. Why not listen to the original and remind yourself how fresh it sounded? Chuck's guitar tone, a relatively inoffensive and clean sound, is a long way from the overdriven versions that subsequently came from Jimi Hendrix and a multitude of other rockers, whose roots lay in 1950s rock'n'roll. Delivered on a big old Gibson ES 335, the choice of axe for jazzers through to rockers and beyond, that key riff never outstays its welcome.

When the legendary Chess label released the song in 1958, it made an immediate impact due to its upbeat tempo and its lyrics about a hot young guitar slinger. Note that its subject, a 'country boy', was initially a 'coloured boy' until Berry realized that American audiences of the day, among whom Neanderthal levels of racism prevailed,

wouldn't react well – and rewrote it. Meanwhile, that line about 'he could play the guitar just like ringing a bell' is one of those illogical but amazing lyrics from rock folklore, which mean nothing but sound great.

MUSICAL LEGACY

There are few better-known songs from the original rock'n'roll era than 'Johnny B Goode', and as a result it has never fallen into obscurity. In popular culture it has crossed over to many spheres of influence, from Jimi Hendrix's beefed-up cover of the song in the late 1960s, when overdrive and amplification technology had evolved to the point where the original recording's slightly timid guitar tones could be replaced with bigger sounds, to its appearance in the Michael J. Fox film *Back To The Future* in 1985. Its simple 12-bar structure and relatively unchallenging guitar parts make it a staple among many amateur bands, and its near-universal appeal has meant that artists as diverse as Peter Tosh and Judas Priest have covered it over the years. When Chuck was inducted into the Rock And Roll Hall Of Fame in 1986, he played a set including 'Johnny B Goode' backed by none other than Bruce Springsteen and his band.

GENRES

Rock'n'roll

RECORDED

1958 in Chicago

PRODUCER

Little 'Bongo' Kraus

BAND MEMBERS

Chuck Berry, Lafayette Leake, Willie Dixon, Fred Below

ON YOUTUBE  http://flametr.com/johnny-b-goode

Scan to see a video on your smartphone (incl. iPhone & Android)

BLACK SABBATH

N.I.B.

Although there isn't really much doubt among educated headbangers that Black Sabbath were the first heavy metal band, a listen to 'N.I.B.' (named after the shape of drummer Bill Ward's goatee beard, which the rest of the band thought was shaped like a pen nib, only gaining the erroneous extension of 'Nativity In Black' some years later) reveals just how close the competition for that title was. The opening riff, played by bassist Geezer Butler after a blues-indebted bass solo, is not significantly heavier or indeed more 'metal' than contemporary hard rock riffs recorded by Led Zeppelin and Deep Purple. Guitarist Tony Iommi's tone is warm, with an analogue fuzz that is light years away from the treated, downtuned tone that he and other metal guitarists used in later years. In fact, a couple of years earlier, Jimi Hendrix was using a similar sound, itself barely much heavier than The Beatles' guitar tone on their 1968 hit 'Revolution'. It's a demonstration, in effect, that heavy music evolved slowly rather than leaping fully formed from the drawer marked Black Sabbath, although the song and its core riffs have lost none of their power over the decades.

GENRES

Heavy metal

RECORDED

1969 in London

PRODUCER

Rodger Bain

BAND MEMBERS

Ozzy Osbourne, Tony Iommi, Geezer Butler, Bill Ward

ON YOUTUBE  http://flametr.com/n-i-b

Scan to see a video on your smartphone (incl. iPhone & Android)

BLACK SABBATH

PARANOID

It's a funny old game, heavy metal. Although Brummie foursome Black Sabbath were the first true heavy metal band out of the blocks, their best-known song to this day – 'Paranoid' – is not really metallic at all. It's catchy, melodic and even poppy to an extent, based on a lightweight riff and containing lyrics that are thought-provoking rather than threatening. 'Finished with my woman, 'cause she couldn't help me with my mind!' warbled Ozzy Osbourne, mostly succeeding in following Tony Iommi's simple, down-stroked riff with his vocal line. If there's a more iconic opening line than that in heavy music, please advise.

RECORDING AND RELEASE

Iommi came up with the main riff during a quick break in the recording of the *Paranoid* album, scarcely intending to turn it into a song and completely unaware – as is so often the case – that it would form one of his band's signature recordings. The secret of its appeal lies in the nifty three-note turnaround after each line, coupled with Geezer Butler's bass fill. In addition, 'Paranoid' is fast-paced and boasts a simple arrangement, making it catchy enough for 1970s postmen to whistle while walking up garden paths each morning – a key indicator in those far-off days of a song's penetration into everyday culture. Released with 'The Wizard' as its B-side, the single reached No. 4 on the UK chart and played a major role in establishing Sabbath – still only two years into their career – as a serious band with commercial clout.

All these years later, 'Paranoid' isn't going anywhere it seems. In some European countries it has transcended the heavy metal genre entirely to become one of those songs routinely requested at cover bands gigs and at

sports events. Black Sabbath themselves have rarely come up with songs that are equivalently memorable, although their self-titled song and 'War Pigs' come close.

MUSICAL LEGACY

The list of artists who have covered the track is long, with especially memorable versions coming from Megadeth (who covered it for the *Nativity In Black* tribute album in 1994), Type O Negative, whose doomy, downtuned version suited their attitude of professional miserablism to a T, and even pop-punk poppets Green Day, who sometimes play it live. This single's fame isn't confined to metal and punk bands, either. There seems to be no shortage of bands from all shades of the rock spectrum who are interested in a spot of polite headbanging. Point your mouse at YouTube and you'll encounter excellent versions of the song by desert-rockers Queens Of The Stone Age, who played it at an awards ceremony in 2007; Scottish pop act Big Country, whose interest in bagpipe-heavy anthems would seem to preclude an interest in 1970s heavy music; maverick publisher Adam Parfrey of the Feral House imprint, who covered it in a solo show; and even an old German *schläger* act called Cindy Und Bert. You couldn't make it up.

GENRES

Heavy metal

PRODUCER

Rodger Bain

RECORDED

1970 in London

BAND MEMBERS

Ozzy Osbourne, Tony Iommi, Geezer Butler, Bill Ward

ON YOUTUBE  http://flametr.com/paranoid-black

Scan to see a video on your smartphone (incl. iPhone & Android)

BLACK SABBATH

IRON MAN

Interviewed a few years back, Opeth frontman Mikael Åkerfeldt, who has made a career out of heavy and interesting music, remembered his first childhood encounter with the music of Black Sabbath, saying 'The first time I heard 'Iron Man', it scared the hell out of me. The voice which starts it is absolutely terrifying, and then that riff starts….' He was right on all counts.

This tale of a time-travelling philosopher, an amusing concept now in the blockbuster era, begins with Ozzy Osbourne's malevolent shriek of 'I am Iron Man!' and Tony Iommi's unnerving string bends, before embarking on a splendidly crafted riff that has gone down in metal history. As with so many of Black Sabbath's best-known songs, Ozzy's vocal melody is in unison with the main riff, a trick that Sabbath employed on many occasions before Ozzy was replaced by the more musically literate Ronnie James Dio in 1979.

RECORDING AND RELEASE

In 1970 Black Sabbath were in the first flush of their creativity, with Iommi and bassist Geezer Butler creating riffs and lyrics at a rapid pace. Many of their early songs have long since passed into rock mythology, among them 'Iron Man'. When the song was written, Osbourne remarked that Iommi's elephantine riff sounded (you'll have to imagine the Brummie monotone here) like 'a great big iron bloke walking around'. An edit of that suggestion for commercial reasons, and 'Iron Man' was born. Recorded swiftly, like so much early metal, the song was issued immediately after 'Paranoid', with 'Electric Funeral' as its B-side.

MUSICAL LEGACY

It took 30 years for the music industry to recognize the stature of 'Iron Man', with the Grammys board awarding the song Best Metal Performance for a live version in 2000. However, metal fans and the wider music-consuming community were far less sluggish, making the song one of Sabbath's most played on the radio and performed in live shows for a good three decades before the Grammy panel woke up to its considerable presence. It helped, of course, that the song has been used in many arenas of creativity, perhaps most prominently in the Marvel superhero films of the same name. Elsewhere, you'll hear 'Iron Man' in the most unexpected places. William 'The Toupee' Shatner covered the song, assisted by Ozzy's ex-guitar player Zakk Wylde, for his *Seeking Major Tom* album in 2011. The Cardigans, who many readers will remember as a fey indie-pop outfit from Sweden, covered 'Iron Man' back in 1996. Irish rockers Therapy? recorded it for *Nativity In Black* in 1994, assisted by Ozzy on vocals (at the time Sabbath were two years away from re-forming; perhaps the old wailer was feeling nostalgic?). You'll also hear the riff sampled by rapper Kanye West in a song called 'Hell Of A Life'. As always, hip-hop and metal managed to complement each other, even when the artists concerned are separated by three decades.

GENRES

Heavy metal

RECORDED

1970 in London

PRODUCER

Rodger Bain

BAND MEMBERS

Ozzy Osbourne, Tony Iommi, Geezer Butler, Bill Ward

ON YOUTUBE  http://flametr.com/iron-man-black

Scan to see a video on your smartphone (incl. iPhone & Android)

BLOC PARTY

HUNTING FOR WITCHES

The high-register riff that you can hear after the electronic intro of 'Hunting For Witches' sounded like the future of guitar music when the song was released in 2007. Although it's mixed relatively low in the overall sound, there's no denying its catchiness. Coupled with a post-punk bass part of great economy and electro layers from a variety of sampled and played sources, 'Hunting For Witches' pierced the consciousness of a new generation of indie listeners for whom Oasis were too old and Kasabian too predictable. The lyrics smacked of current affairs, referencing the control that the media enjoys over the populace in times of unrest; such as the 7/7 bombings which occurred before the single's release. For a while there, Bloc Party were the *NME*'s favourite new band, helped along by singer Kele Okereke's fondness for a soundbite, although their stock seems to have fallen in subsequent years. Still, they'll always have this clever bit of riffery to their name.

GENRES

Indie rock, post-punk revival, electropunk

RECORDED

2006 in Westmeath, Ireland and London

PRODUCER

Jacknife Lee

BAND MEMBERS

Kele Okereke, Russell Lissack, Gordon Moakes, Matt Tong

ON YOUTUBE http://flametr.com/hunting-witches

Scan to see a video on your smartphone (incl. iPhone & Android)

BLUE ÖYSTER CULT

(DON'T FEAR) THE REAPER

In July 1976 punk and disco were about to become huge global forces within popular music, but for many American radio listeners, all that really mattered was rock with a capital R. Bands like Led Zeppelin, Aerosmith and Ted Nugent had filled stadiums through the 1970s with monolithic, anthemic songs, and no song came bigger or more profound that summer than '(Don't Fear) The Reaper'. Constructed around Blue Öyster Cult guitarist Donald 'Buck Dharma' Roeser's drone riff in A minor, and devolving into distinct sections, each with its own dynamic, the song addressed the eternal themes of love, death and the importance of a lengthy guitar solo. In the years since, the song has become a mighty symbol of Americana, up there with 'Hotel California' or 'Cat Scratch Fever', despite several spins of the wheel of fashion. In fact, '(Don't Fear) The Reaper' is neither fashionable nor unfashionable. Like the Hollywood sign or the four presidents on the face of Mount Rushmore, it is simply there, and no doubt will always be. Thus is once more demonstrated the eternal power of a good riff.

GENRES

Hard rock, psychedelic rock

RECORDED

1976 in New York

PRODUCERS

David Lucas, Murray Krugman, Sandy Pearlman

BAND MEMBERS

Donald 'Buck Dharma' Roeser, Eric Bloom, Alan Lanier, Joe Bouchard, Albert Bouchard

Scan to see a video on your smartphone (incl. iPhone & Android)

BLUR

SONG 2

'Woo-hoo!' we all sang in April 1997 when cheeky mockneys Blur released their second single from their self-titled fifth album. Coming as 'Song 2' did on the heels of the lo-fi 'Beetlebum', it was a breath of fresh air, largely because of the giant guitar riff that propelled it. Layering his guitars with a warm overdrive and plenty of bottom end, hardcore punk enthusiast Graham Coxon came as close as the British indie scene has ever come to creating a genuine wall of sound. Meanwhile, singer Damon Albarn overlaid the riff with that irritating but catchy falsetto, pretty much ensuring that metalheads and indie kids alike pricked up their ears when they heard the song. It's been used in dozens of sporting TV broadcasts and ad spots ever since – an ironically successful performance for a song that purported to be taking the mickey out of heavy music. Instead, it redefined heaviness for a generation of Britpoppers, gaining Blur their first large American audiences at the same time. God knows what US crowds thought when the band played 'Country House' and 'Parklife' at them though.

GENRES

Alternative rock, grunge

RECORDED

1996 in Reykjavik and London

PRODUCER

Stephen Street

BAND MEMBERS

Damon Albarn, Graham Coxon, Alex James, Dave Rowntree

ON YOUTUBE  http://flametr.com/song-2-blur

Scan to see a video on your smartphone (incl. iPhone & Android)

CALIFORNIA
86

DAVID BOWIE

REBEL REBEL

Glam rock was in full swing in 1974 when this signature song by the erstwhile Davey Jones hit the charts. This was an era of regrettable sartorial and musical fashions in many ways, when builders called Clive from Slough would dress up in skintight lurex, call themselves Dayglo Dave and play watered-down Sweet covers in working men's clubs. Our man Bowie largely avoided these errors, carving himself an image somewhere between visiting alien and demon mullet-wearer with wonky eyes, and to this day his glam-era material is worth your time, 'Rebel Rebel' in particular, which was effectively his last foray into the genre. The opening riff, with its top-heavy overdrive and tinkling arpeggiated chord, is instantly recognizable, even if the amp and effect he's using on it sound as if they cost tuppence.

RECORDING AND RELEASE

Released with 'Queen Bitch' on its B-side, 'Rebel Rebel' rapidly became an anthem for a young, mid-1970s audience who were rapidly outgrowing glam. Pop music was becoming a harder, more demanding beast and the song fitted the demands of a fanbase who wanted no reminders of the softer, more indulgent sounds of the 1960s.

Musically, the song was all Bowie's; the parent album, *Diamond Dogs*, was the first major hit that he'd recorded without long-time guitarist cohort Mick Ronson. It suffered not a jot for Ronno's absence. Indeed, critics noted a new, Rolling Stones-indebted, blues-rock style to that opening riff which had previously been absent from Bowie's work. The US release featured a different and less digestible mix, but was withdrawn soon afterwards and replaced with the familiar honky-tonk song that is still famous today.

MUSICAL LEGACY

Check out one of the many live versions of 'Rebel Rebel' that exist. There's a reason why the song is such a popular choice for inclusion in Bowie's live set. The moment that instantly recognizable riff kicks in, audiences love it. It is a genuinely moving moment in a set full of such moments. His 2010 double live album, *A Reality Tour*, begins with this song. Note that after the initial bars, Bowie (or his musical director) delay the opening of the full song, inciting the audience to join him in the song's opening lines.

Meanwhile, the list of musicians and groups who have covered 'Rebel Rebel' beggars belief. Just some of this stellar cast includes Bryan Adams, Def Leppard, Duran Duran, Joan Jett & The Blackhearts, Manic Street Preachers, Sigue Sigue Sputnik, The Smashing Pumpkins and even various crowds of Manchester United soccer fans, who are said to have sung 'Neville, Neville' to the famous melody in honour of their defenders Phil and Gary Neville. Truly, a song for all seasons, and reflective of its creator, who has donned and discarded more performing identities than most artists would dare to consider in a lifetime.

GENRES

Glam rock

RECORDED

1974 in Hilversum, The Netherlands

PRODUCER

David Bowie

BAND MEMBERS

David Bowie, Herbie Flowers, Mike Garson, Aynsley Dunbar

http://flametr.com/rebel-rebel-bowie

Scan to see a video on your smartphone (incl. iPhone & Android)

EDDIE COCHRAN

SUMMERTIME BLUES

You were doomed to disappointment if you were a teenager with a rebellious streak before the mid-1950s. In fact, the concept of 'teenager' hadn't really been invented at this point, largely because kids didn't have any money and therefore politicians and corporations ignored them. After Elvis emerged with his hips a-swivelling in 1956, however, things began to change, and even though teens were still dismissed, they at least had something to listen to that wasn't sung by a nauseating crooner or an ancient jazz bore. Rockabilly was the name of the game, and when Eddie Cochran appeared with the amazing 'Summertime Blues', the future started to look a little brighter. This song, perhaps more so than any other from the era, was an extended middle finger directly in the face of authority, whoever that might be – your parents, your teachers and quite possibly your boss.

RECORDING AND RELEASE

'Summertime Blues' was written by Cochran and his manager Jerry Capehart and is a devastatingly effective composition. A classic 12-bar blues in an era when the new rockabilly sound incorporated few other song structures, the song is anchored by the bass and drum parts and embellished with the full sound of Cochran's Gretsch. His moderately harsh vocals – surely a shock to many listeners in the era of Sinatra and Crosby? – are mixed high, making it clear that if 'Summertime Blues' is about anything, it is about the anger of a young kid forced to do what his dad and grandpa did before him; in other words, leave school at 15 in order to work a mind-numbing job in a factory for 45 years. This is the sound of distilled, teenage rancour, and still sounds that way, even after decades of rebellious youth. It was released on the Liberty label with 'Love Again' on the flip side and, in terms of classic rock'n'roll, is up there with Sun-era Elvis Presley.

MUSICAL LEGACY

Doesn't every kid in a band have a go at 'Summertime Blues' at some point, along with Chuck Berry's 'Johnny B Goode'? Covers of this immortal song are too numerous to count, but let's doff the cap to two notable versions by Blue Cheer and The Who. If you know anything about either band, you'll know that the song was played at massive volume and often dragged out on stage into a lengthy jam. As both groups were hailed at various times as one of the very first heavy metal bands, it's not surprising that they chose this song to jam along to – it's simple, to the point and easy to play.

As for Eddie Cochran himself, he didn't live long enough to see either cover version make it onto vinyl. In 1960, at only 22 years of age, he died in a taxi crash in the English county of Wiltshire. He achieved immortality, however, both because his songs have endured and because memories of people who die young endure.

GENRES

Rockabilly

RECORDED

1958

PRODUCER

Eddie Cochran

BAND MEMBERS

Eddie Cochran, Connie Smith, Earl Palmer

ON YOUTUBE  http://flametr.com/summertime-blues

Scan to see a video on your smartphone (incl. iPhone & Android)

GRETSCH

CREAM

SUNSHINE OF YOUR LOVE

'Cream were always an experimental jazz trio,' said Jack Bruce in 2003, adding with a chuckle, 'We just didn't tell Eric.' The veteran bassist had a point. Cream could well have been the first band to claim the 'progressive rock' tag, given the pool of blues, jazz, rock and world influences from which the three mercurial musicians drank. This song, one of the threesome's most enduring along with 'White Room', begins with that unforgettable descending riff, composed of seven notes played nine times, before heading off in a direction that is one part acid rock and another part blues workout. Listen carefully and you'll notice Ginger Baker's African-influenced drums and also that the first phrase of Eric Clapton's guitar solo comes from the vocal line of the old ballad 'Blue Moon'. In doing this, he set up a witty contrast between the sun and the moon of the two song-titles. Those crazy 1960s cats.

RECORDING AND RELEASE

'Sunshine Of Your Love' was written by Bruce and lyricist Pete Brown, supposedly after a night on the tiles, which included taking in a gig by Cream's contemporary, Jimi Hendrix. As Bruce strolled through the opening line on a double bass, Brown looked out of the window, noticed the rising sun and wrote the lyric 'It's getting near dawn / The lights close their tired eyes….' Do lights have eyes? Either way, the song quickly took shape, with Clapton contributing the bridge ('I've been waiting so long') and a beautiful solo on a Gibson SG. The song was released with 'SWLABR' (what do you mean, you didn't know it stands for 'She Walks Like A Bearded Rainbow'?) and inspired several significant cover versions.

MUSICAL LEGACY

Jimi Hendrix, as we see elsewhere in this book, was prone to taking other artists' songs, performing them live and overdriven, and extending them into blues jams. He made a point of doing this with 'Sunshine Of Your Love', which he recorded several times (see YouTube, Spotify or even one of those old-fashioned CD things such as *Winterland*) and turned into an event. The range of musicians who covered 'Sunshine ...' is both wide and varied, stretching from British electro-punks Fudge Tunnel, via funkmasters Blood, Sweat & Tears and Frank Zappa, to stoner-rock drummer Brant Bjork, ex of Kyuss. Perhaps most remarkably, Ella Fitzgerald – whose career in jazz would undoubtedly have influenced Bruce, if not the rest of Cream – covered 'Sunshine Of Your Love' in 1968, the year after its original release. She evidently saw something in this group of white British hippies that more traditional jazzers did not. Cream themselves were too volatile to stay together for long, and after three years and four albums, they split in 1969. Bruce and Baker took up eclectic solo careers in world music and jazz fusion, while Clapton refined a form of huge-selling blues pop and sold millions. A reunion in 2005 was executed with dignity, leaving Cream's still-huge fanbase wanting more. This desire is unlikely to be fulfilled, but those early Cream songs will live on forever.

GENRES

Psychedelic rock, blues rock, acid rock

RECORDED

1967 in New York

PRODUCER

Felix Pappalardi

BAND MEMBERS

Jack Bruce, Eric Clapton, Ginger Baker

ON YOUTUBE  http://flametr.com/sunshine-cream

Scan to see a video on your smartphone (incl. iPhone & Android)

CREEDENCE CLEARWATER REVIVAL

UP AROUND THE BEND

String-skipping like a madman, Creedence Clearwater Revival guitarist John Fogerty delivered this wailing opening riff, and in so doing created a classic, showstopping live moment. Like a country hoedown combined with the best laid-back FM rock that 1970s America could muster, 'Up Around The Bend' was an instant favourite with fans. Note that his more civilized solo echoes that opening line, doing that clever thing that all the best lead guitarists do of telling a song within a song. On its release, 'Up Around The Bend' reached No. 4 on the *Billboard* singles chart and eventually sold over a million copies. Since then the song has appeared on several soundtracks, in the *Guitar Hero World Tour* video game, and as a notable cover by Finnish glam-metal band Hanoi Rocks. Elton John also made a habit of covering the song live, adapting it for his patented ivories-tinkling style. All these years later, Creedence Clearwater Revival are perhaps better known for the iconic 'Bad Moon Rising', but 'Up Around The Bend' remains the song of choice for Fogerty enthusiasts.

GENRES

Roots rock

RECORDED

1970 in San Francisco

PRODUCER

John Fogerty

BAND MEMBERS

John Fogerty, Tom Fogerty, Stu Cook, Doug Clifford

Scan to see a video on your smartphone (incl. iPhone & Android)

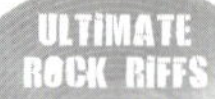

THE DARKNESS

I BELIEVE IN A THING CALLED LOVE

Glam metal, in the Cinderella, Warrant and Poison sense, was dead in the water in 2003, when headbangers were just emerging from the wreckage of the nu-metal movement. The Darkness chose their moment perfectly, releasing their debut album *Permission To Land* just when metal fans were looking for something a bit more cheerful than Limp Bizkit. Like the aforementioned hair bands, the Lincolnshire foursome offered up a slick blend of album-oriented rock influences (Journey, Boston and Aerosmith among them), added some silly humour and catsuits, and reaped enormous rewards. The opening riff of 'I Believe In A Thing Called Love' begins at a lo-fi whisper before erupting into a beast that defies the listener not to leap up and whip out an air guitar. After a second album, the band split due to drug abuse on the part of singer Justin Hawkins. There followed a few years of so-so side projects, and then The Darkness got clean, sober and fit, patched up their differences, re-formed in 2011 and are back doing big business once more.

GENRES

Hard rock, glam metal

RECORDED

2003 in South Thoresby, Lincolnshire and London

PRODUCER

Pedro Ferreira

BAND MEMBERS

Justin Hawkins, Dan Hawkins, Frankie Poullain, Ed Graham

Scan to see a video on your smartphone (incl. iPhone & Android)

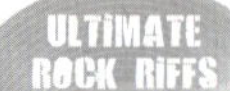

DEEP PURPLE

SMOKE ON THE WATER

'Smoke On The Water' should be celebrated for two reasons. Firstly, it has *that* riff, which we'll come to shortly. Secondly, it deserves a prize from the Plain English Campaign, thanks to its helpfully literal lyrics which detail a visit made by Deep Purple's most profitable line-up, Mark II, to Switzerland. The band had visited Montreux, near Lake Geneva ('We all came out to Montreux, on the Lake Geneva shoreline') in order to record a new album in a mobile studio without delay ('to make records with a mobile, we didn't have much time'). See? Add to this the immortal chorus line about a fire near the lake ('Smo-o-oke on the water!') and there really isn't much room for misinterpretation. As for that opening riff – lest we forget, a simple march through A, C, D, A, C, D, E♭ – it's one of those patterns that you hear once and you never forget ... largely because every guitar store in the world has someone playing it.

RECORDING AND RELEASE

Recorded with Blackmore's usual white Fender Stratocaster, the opening riff of 'Smoke ...' is played in two-string chords made up of root-plus-fourth, rather than power chords made up of the usual root-plus-fifth. Try the two versions: they sound completely different. Organist Jon Lord played the riff in unison on a Hammond G3 through an overdriven guitar amp to make up Purple's signature sound. Together, they pretty much defined the tone of an entire genre of early-1970s bombastic rock. As is so often the case with these epoch-shaping songs, neither Blackmore nor Lord had any inkling when they wrote 'Smoke On The Water' that it would become such a huge hit for decades to come. In fact, the song was not intended to be a single at first, and only came out a year after the parent album,

Machine Head, had become a hit in its own right. When the song appeared, it was significant that its B-side was a live version of the same song, which had become a live favourite among Purple fans in the months since its appearance.

MUSICAL LEGACY

Between 1994 and 2009, several attempts took place to gather many thousands of guitarists and have them play the riff to 'Smoke On The Water' simultaneously, thus breaking a *Guinness Book Of Records* world standard. Why this song in particular? After all, there are simpler riffs to play – Eddie Cochran's 'Summertime Blues', Norman Greenbaum's 'Spirit In The Sky', Black Sabbath's 'Black Sabbath' and The Doors' 'Roadhouse Blues' all come to mind – even if you permit the record-breaking guitar crowd to play the 'Smoke …' riff with power chords, the more usual method. But no – 'Smoke On The Water' is a classic. Everyone knows it. It epitomizes rock and, in all probability, it always will. The song also appears on more movie soundtracks than we can mention here, and has been covered by a plethora of groups from 'Weird Al' Yankovic to Black Sabbath, who played a heavier version of the song when Ian Gillan joined them for the *Born Again* album in 1983.

GENRES

Hard rock, psychedelic rock, heavy metal

RECORDED

1971 in Montreux, Switzerland

PRODUCER

Deep Purple

BAND MEMBERS

Ian Gillan, Ritchie Blackmore, Roger Glover, Jon Lord, Ian Paice

ON YOUTUBE  http://flametr.com/smoke-on-water

Scan to see a video on your smartphone (incl. iPhone & Android)

DEREK & THE DOMINOS

LAYLA

Unrequited love as an emotional song theme is usually associated with pale indie musicians in need of a good meal, and rarely (if ever) inspires songs raunchier than a morose acoustic ballad. However, in the case of 'Layla', composer Eric Clapton's unresolved affection for 1960s model and 'face' Pattie Boyd led to a fully leaded blues-rock workout that remains a staple of many a *100 Percent Driving Rock Anthems For Dads* CD to this day. The small matter of Pattie being married to Eric's buddy George Harrison, of up-and-coming Scouse beat combo The Beatles, was apparently beside the point. At least old Slowhand dug out a pseudonym for the song from Arabian legend, rather than calling the song 'Pattie' and causing no end of embarrassment at Surrey cocktail parties at the tail-end of the 1960s.

RECORDING AND RELEASE

That opening riff, executed on two strings by Eric, backed up by two more guitar tracks and then counterpointed by Duane Allman's higher-register version, is instantly recognizable. It is Allman who is said to have upgraded the song into a rock composition, with Eric having originally composed it as a ballad. Indeed, the 1993 acoustic version which won awards on the back of the *Eric Clapton Unplugged* album was precisely that. Now, the unique selling point of 'Layla' is that it is composed of two distinct movements: the original rocked-up guitar piece and then a piano coda composed by fellow Domino Peter Gordon. This latter section allows both Clapton and Allman to layer guitar solo tracks over and over again, with the end result a wondrous collage of intermeshed melodies. You'll hear Allman playing extremely high notes with a guitar slide, a technique not often used in mainstream rock music.

MUSICAL LEGACY

'Layla' did the trick. Eventually Eric confessed his desire for Pattie to George Harrison, who is said to have received the news with relatively good grace. When Pattie and George split up, Eric was there as a shoulder for Pattie to cry on and the rest is history. The song itself was less successful as a commercial single, largely because Eric's name didn't appear on the front of the Derek & The Dominos' album *Layla And Other Assorted Love Songs* (record companies and their infinite wisdom, eh?). Then again, when Eric released a solo best-of collection called *The History Of Eric Clapton* in 1972, 'Layla' got the attention it deserved and became a Top 10 single. Even this was nothing compared to the riotous response the song received when the unplugged version came out in the 1990s. It famously beat Nirvana's 'Smells Like Teen Spirit' for the Best Rock Song Grammy award in 1992, a pretty bizarre decision given the latter song's global impact at the time. Although the Grammy judges were made to look massively out of touch as a result, there's no denying the power of 'Layla' to this day, plugged-in or otherwise.

GENRES

Blues rock

RECORDED

1970 in Miami

PRODUCER

Tom Dowd, Derek & The Dominos

BAND MEMBERS

Eric Clapton, Duane Allman, Peter Gordon, Carl Radle, Bobby Whitlock

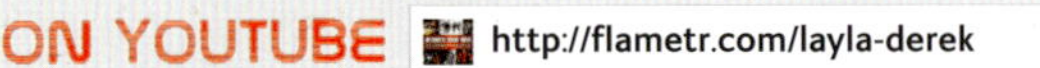

Scan to see a video on your smartphone (incl. iPhone & Android)

DIRE STRAITS

MONEY FOR NOTHING

When Dire Straits' signature song 'Money For Nothing' was released in June 1985, by chance only three weeks before the biggest rock concert in history, something was in the air. Artists had begun to take advantage of the existence of MTV, then three years old in America but still two years away from its arrival in the UK and Europe. Rock was becoming global as artists began to associate their platforms with political and environmental issues. Things were getting bigger, slicker and shinier, literally in the case of the then-new compact disc technology, which somehow epitomized the 1980s. For a generation of music consumers, CDs, MTV, Live Aid and 'Money For Nothing' – plus a cabal of huge-earning, politically concerned musicians like Phil Collins, Eric Clapton, Peter Gabriel, Simple Minds and Sting – became associated with a kind of giant leap forward. It was the moment when rock went corporate in the public eye, although in reality it had been a corporate affair since at least 1960.

RECORDING AND RELEASE

And all because of a riff and a video. 'Money For Nothing' begins with a crescendo of drums and keyboards, plus Sting (who had arrived at Dire Straits' Montserrat recording studio to say hello) singing the chorus melody of The Police's 'Don't Stand So Close To Me' but with the words 'I want my MTV'. This segues into frontman Mark Knopfler's fingerpicked blues riff, a heavily overdriven figure that is accompanied by the rest of the band after a single run-through. Knopfler's lyrics – sung from the perspective of a blue-collar manual worker who sees a pop star on MTV and envies him for his 'money for nothing and chicks for free' lifestyle – became mildly controversial in later years because of the word 'faggot', despite Knopfler's protestations that he was singing in character. Indeed, the lyrics

were inspired by a delivery staff member whom Knopfler had encountered in a 'custom kitchen' store, watching MTV on a bank of televisions and commenting on the singer, saying apparently without irony 'That ain't working'. Guitar buffs will be interested to hear that Knopfler attempted to base his famous guitar sound in 'Money For Nothing' on the tone used by ZZ Top's legendary axeman Billy Gibbons, even going as far as to use a wah pedal rocked to a halfway position, just as Gibbons had done.

MUSICAL LEGACY

Thanks to its No. 1 chart positions around the world and most particularly in the USA, where its CGI-heavy video was an unprecedented hit, 'Money For Nothing' has entered the rock'n'roll vocabulary. Both video and song were parodied by the unaccountably successful comedian 'Weird Al' Yankovic and, in the UK, by the infamous satirical sketch show *Spitting Image*, which featured a puppet of Sting singing 'I want my royalties'. Dire Straits, who have been on hiatus since the late 1990s while Knopfler pursues a solo career and composes film soundtracks, played the song repeatedly on their latterday tours and at the various worthy festivals and concerts which followed in the wake of Live Aid.

GENRES

Roots rock, new wave

RECORDED

1984 in Montserrat, West Indies

PRODUCER

Mark Knopfler, Neil Dorfsman

BAND MEMBERS

Mark Knopfler, John Illsley, Alan Clark, Guy Fletcher, Omar Hakim, Terry Williams

ON YOUTUBE  http://flametr.com/money-for

Scan to see a video on your smartphone (incl. iPhone & Android)

THE DOORS

ROADHOUSE BLUES

While The Doors are known for any number of songs – 'Break On Through (To The Other Side)', 'LA Woman', 'Riders On The Storm' and 'The End' among them – in terms of riffs, their most recognizable work is undoubtedly 'Roadhouse Blues'. This 1970 song, released as the B-side of 'You Make Me Real', is composed of a simple pedalled note and turnaround, played by guitarist Robbie Krieger before the rest of the band (plus studio 'help' in the original version) join him. It's a highly effective blues stomp, explaining its subsequent usage in decades to come on various film soundtracks, as well as the many cover versions that have been recorded. Numerous club and cover bands will also play the song at any given event, largely because as a live jam it's usually an excellent choice. Anyone who remembers the Jeff Healey Band's version in the seminal 1989 cheese flick *Road House* will understand its appeal.

RECORDING AND RELEASE

It's uncertain which of the guitar tracks laid down in the studio for the original version of 'Roadhouse Blues', recorded for the *Morrison Hotel* album in 1969, made it to the final cut, as Robbie Krieger was joined by Elektra's in-house guitarist Lonnie Mack in the studio. That hooky opening riff is all Krieger's, though, and was an instant pull to Doors audiences on *Morrison Hotel*'s release. The Doors went on to play the song regularly for the remainder of their career, which effectively ended with Jim Morrison's death in July 1971. However, when the surviving members regrouped as The Doors Of The 21st Century, with Cult singer Ian Astbury, for a run of dates that lasted from 2002 to 2007 (longer, in fact, than their original career), the song was reborn and played in all its former glory.

MUSICAL LEGACY

Classic songs never die – they simply appear and re-appear in a multitude of mixes and formats. The first wave of Doors reissues featuring 'Roadhouse Blues' came in the late 1990s, with a 1997 four-CD box set called (appropriately) *The Doors: Box Set* and then another called *The Complete Studio Recordings* two years later. A bespoke record label called Bright Midnight was launched in 2000, specifically to handle the issue of new Morrison-era Doors albums, which is where you went if you wanted a serious number of 'Roadhouse Blues' versions. In 2006 we were offered DVD-Audio and DTS discs in the *Perception* collection. Warner Brothers' reissue division Rhino also upped its game, issuing *Live In Boston* (2007), *Pittsburgh Civic Arena* (2008), *Live At The Matrix 1967* (2008), *Live In New York* (the final four Morrison-era concerts on six discs, 2009), *Live In Vancouver 1970* (2010), *A Collection* (2011) and *Live At The Bowl '68* (2012). It never stops. Keep an ear out for a live version of 'Roadhouse Blues' on *An American Prayer*, *In Concert* and *Greatest Hits*, on which Jim can be heard exchanging banter with a female audience member. It was hailed by some critics as the ultimate live version, extending into an awe-inspiring blues-rock workout.

GENRES

Blues rock, boogie rock

RECORDED

1969 in Los Angeles

PRODUCER

Paul A. Rothchild

BAND MEMBERS

Jim Morrison, Robbie Krieger, Ray Manzarek, John Densmore

ON YOUTUBE  http://flametr.com/roadhouse-blues

Scan to see a video on your smartphone (incl. iPhone & Android)

THE EAGLES

LIFE IN THE FAST LANE

Released in May 1977, when Eagles fever was at its height in America, 'Life In The Fast Lane' was a whole new approach to country rock. Fast, dynamic and exciting, the song (and the nifty riff by guitarist extraordinaire Joe Walsh that starts it) was a far cry from the nasal strumming which country listeners had come to expect. The song also proved to be a perfect buzz of adrenaline when played on the parent album, the 16-times platinum-selling *Hotel California*. Placed after the mellow 'New Kid In Town', 'Life In The Fast Lane' proved that The Eagles were no mere stoners. Indeed, this was cocaine music, as referenced in the album's title track. The song's enduring appeal was demonstrated as late as 2000 by its use, ironic or otherwise, as a sample in rap-metallers Limp Bizkit's 'Livin' It Up', and covers from country artists prove its continued popularity in that particular huge-selling arena. Quite simply, when The Eagles, perpetually at war with each other in their 1970s incarnation, played the song, the American Dream seemed a reality.

GENRE

Hard rock

RECORDED

1976 in Miami and Los Angeles

PRODUCER

Bill Szymczyk

BAND MEMBERS

Glenn Frey, Don Henley, Randy Meisner, Don Felder, Joe Walsh

http://flametr.com/fast-lane-eagles

Scan to see a video on your smartphone (incl. iPhone & Android)

FRANZ FERDINAND

TAKE ME OUT

There was something edgy about 'Take Me Out' when it appeared in January 2004. Perhaps it's because stripped-down, post-punk rock music from the drawer marked 'Talking Heads' and 'The Strokes' – with a dash of homegrown Scottish rawness thrown in – could only sound cool. Maybe it's that persuasive riff, a simple staccato job that kicks in after the intro, a long build-up of layered guitars, gives way. Undoubtedly it's the relentless way that 'Take Me Out' sticks to its groove, anchored solidly by overdriven Telecaster tones and a simple, stabbing bass-line. Once it has sucked you in, 'Take Me Out' refuses to let you go. As the second single from the Glasgow foursome, it represented Alex Kapranos and his band at the peak of their youthful powers. Since then, they've grown to the status of an internationally headlining band, as well as reminding us all that truly cool men flirt with moustaches from time to time. Have they equalled that mighty riff? Not yet, but there's still plenty of time for them to write 'Take Me Out Part 2'.

GENRE

Indie rock, post-punk revival

RECORDED

2003 in Malmö, Sweden

PRODUCER

Tore Johansson

BAND MEMBERS

Alex Kapranos, Nick McCarthy, Bob Hardy, Paul Thomson

ON YOUTUBE  http://flametr.com/take-me-out-franz

Scan to see a video on your smartphone (incl. iPhone & Android)

Franz

FREE

ALL RIGHT NOW

Anchored by not one but two amazing riffs, one of them on a bass, 'All Right Now' will forever be the song for which blues-rock quartet Free are remembered. The opening figure, a starkly overdriven riff in fourths with a ringing tail, sets out the 1970 song's stall with great economy and groove, enticing at least two generations since then to get up and boogie. The latter riff, executed by bassist Andy Fraser when the song devolves into its second half, is a slinky little fingerstyle number plus descending chord that is rapidly overlaid by the rest of the band, who ride the groove until the end. If you were lucky enough to be at the Isle Of Wight Festival that year, and *compos mentis* at the same time (which is not guaranteed), you'll recall the impact the song had on the hindquarters of the 600,000 people who heard it. It has been covered by a whole range of musicians, from Mike Oldfield to Christina Aguilera – proof of its lasting appeal.

GENRE

Hard rock

RECORDED

1970 in London

PRODUCER

Free

BAND MEMBERS

Paul Rodgers, Paul Kossoff, Andy Fraser, Simon Kirke

ON YOUTUBE  http://flametr.com/all-right-free

Scan to see a video on your smartphone (incl. iPhone & Android)

GREEN DAY

AMERICAN IDIOT

It's hard to imagine now but, in the summer of 2004, Green Day's career was at a low ebb. Their recent albums and singles had seemed a tad lacklustre after the acclaim that pop-punk had enjoyed through the 1990s, and inspiration was thought to have deserted Billie Joe Armstrong and his crew. This turned out to be temporary, fortunately, when Green Day released 'American Idiot', a barnstorming polemic of a song that railed mercilessly against the US administration of the day, the controlling media and America's self-perception as a global police force, over a classic four-chord punk riff. Assisted by a chaotically elegant video, 'American Idiot' and the album with which it shared its name ruled the airwaves throughout the middle of the decade, and reinstated Green Day as a band of vision, not least because the parent album was a conceptual affair of some depth. Eight years later, at the time of writing, Green Day are jostling for position with Metallica and the Foo Fighters as the band that takes most money on tour. Not bad for a bunch of punks.

GENRE

Punk rock

RECORDED

2003–04 in Oakland and Los Angeles

PRODUCER

Rob Cavallo

BAND MEMBERS

Billie Joe Armstrong, Mike Dirnt, Tre Cool

ON YOUTUBE  http://flametr.com/american-idiot

Scan to see a video on your smartphone (incl. iPhone & Android)

GREEN
DAY

THE GUESS WHO

AMERICAN WOMAN

A Guess Who compilation CD was released in the 2000s with liner notes claiming that 'American Woman', the Canadian group's 1970 hit, was one of the greatest songs North America had ever produced. The writer had some grounds for this claim, even if 'American Woman' hardly has the clout of contemporary rock songs by, say, The Eagles or The Doors. It is based on a riff that epitomizes groove-rock in its 1970s incarnation and, what's more, it came to represent the feelings of a generation about America and its role in conflicts such as Vietnam. Given a few spins, 'American Woman' hooks the listener in with its relentless funk-rock groove and refuses to let go – it has that much power.

RECORDING AND RELEASE

The acoustic opening section of 'American Woman' soon morphs into a full-blooded rock workout, with that sublime riff the foundation of literally hundreds of songs to be recorded in years to come. The band hadn't intended it to be perceived as a commentary on Vietnam (despite the line 'I don't want your war machines'), explaining rather that 'American Woman' simply reflected their dismay at touring through major American cities and witnessing urban deprivation. Returning to their home town of Winnipeg to be greeted by the wholesome country ladies they'd known as kids, the band decided to pen a tribute to said females and note in passing the urban horrors they'd seen on their travels. This was to no avail. Listeners immediately interpreted 'American Woman' as a) a lascivious thumbs-up to women in general and b) an attack on the Vietnam draft, which – fortunately for The Guess Who – was not in force in Canada. The band themselves shrugged and explained that song meanings are allocated by listeners after the fact and,

whatever intentions they may have had when they wrote 'American Woman', said intentions would be permanently obscured. Wise words, we reckon, especially as the same sentiments had been expressed just a couple of years before the release of the song by none other than John Lennon.

MUSICAL LEGACY

Lenny Kravitz, the perennial retro-rock revivalist, has recorded the best-known cover of 'American Woman' to date. His version is slower, funkier and less referential to the political implications (intended or otherwise) of the original, with Lenny's obvious focus on the sweet-lovin' women of the title. His cover was used in the soundtrack for the 1999 comedy *Austin Powers: The Spy Who Shagged Me* and scooped a Grammy the following year, a coup that merely reflects the demographic of the Grammy board, if we're being fair. Curiously, Lenny's version omitted the original guitar solo, a decision he explained by saying that he was unable to emulate the correct tone. Given that all of his previous work had been based on a precisely 1970s guitar tone, this claim was a little difficult to swallow, but then again, anyone reading this who has ever struggled with a recalcitrant amp and signal chain will perhaps understand his point.

GENRES

Rock, blues rock, hard rock

RECORDED

1969 in Chicago

PRODUCER

Jack Richardson

BAND MEMBERS

Randy Bachman, Burton Cummings, Garry Peterson, Jim Kale

http://flametr.com/american-woman

Scan to see a video on your smartphone (incl. iPhone & Android)

GUNS N' ROSES

WELCOME TO THE JUNGLE

Guns N' Roses guitarist Saul 'Slash' Hudson, he of the Les Paul and top hat collection, once said that of all the years of the 1980s, 1987 was the most 'Eighties' – in part because his band first began releasing major-label music in that year. He had a point. Few rock bands epitomize the decade of big hair and big shoulderpads more than Guns N' Roses, the hard-partying Hollywood act who billed themselves 'The Most Dangerous Band In The World', perhaps unwisely.

Their debut album, *Appetite For Destruction*, was a shining fluke, much better than the albums that followed, and chock full of songs that begged to be remembered the moment you heard them. The first song, 'Welcome To The Jungle', begins with a delayed guitar stutter before the bass and drums join in, and there's a build-up to the key riff, a brash descending affair that positively reeks of influences such as The New York Dolls and The Sex Pistols.

RECORDING AND RELEASE

Guns N' Roses recorded 'Welcome To The Jungle' in a brainstorming session when they were writing new material for their debut album. The main riff was bassist Duff McKagan's composition; he'd written it for an earlier band and discarded it. Slash played the riff for singer Axl Rose and added new parts. Within three hours, the song was written and arranged. Lyrically, the song deals with Rose's sense of alienation on arriving in California for the first time after a long bus ride from the sticks. He'd previously written a similar song called 'One In A Million', which described the same experience and which had become controversial because of some uncomplimentary terms that he'd applied

419

to LA's residents, but 'Welcome To The Jungle' was gentler, at least lyrically. Musically, the song is a riff storm, pausing for breath briefly in its mid-section before resuming for Slash's wailing solo. The ending, a sudden, vaudeville slam to a halt, sets up the rest of the *Appetite* album with an evil sneer.

MUSICAL LEGACY

The world was keen to buy into the down-at-heel glamour that Guns N' Roses portrayed with their music, helped by the video for 'Welcome To The Jungle', in which Axl – complete with straw in mouth – arrives in LA, only to be approached by Stradlin as an evil drug dealer. Later on, Axl is transformed into an urban punk, all his country naivety gone and accompanying boozehounds like Slash on their adventures. The clip left a permanent mark on America's metal scene and, along with the other big singles from *Appetite*, 'Welcome To The Jungle' is still regularly played on music TV channels. Guns N' Roses routinely play it as the first or second song in their live set, with Axl – the sole remaining original member – obviously aware of its iconic status among fans. Indeed, nostalgia among Guns N' Roses fans for the early era means that a re-formation of the original quintet can only be a matter of time.

GENRES

Heavy metal, hard rock

RECORDED

1987 in Los Angeles

PRODUCER

Mike Clink

BAND MEMBERS

Axl Rose, Slash, Izzy Stradlin, Duff McKagan, Steven Adler

ON YOUTUBE 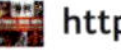 http://flametr.com/welcome-jungle

GUNS N' ROSES

SWEET CHILD O' MINE

By the summer of 1988, Guns N' Roses had made their mark as poutin', headbangin', heavy-metal bad boys from Hollywood, and it was high time for a ballad. 'Sweet Child O' Mine' was the obvious candidate for the next song from their immense debut album, *Appetite For Destruction*, and on its appearance the song made a global impact which has barely abated in the quarter-century since. '

Sweet Child ...' would never have had the public acceptance that it has enjoyed without Slash's ear-grabbing opening riff, which repeats through the choruses. Although the great man has dismissed it on many occasions as either a joke or merely an exercise in string-skipping, he cleared it up in an interview with the author when he said: 'Initially it was just a cool, neat riff that I'd come up with. It was an interesting pattern and it was really melodic, but I don't think I would have presented it to the band and said "Hey, I've got this idea!" – because I just happened to come up with it while we were all hanging around together. Izzy [Stradlin, second guitarist] was the first one to start playing behind it, and once that happened Axl [Rose, singer] started making up words, and it took off that way.'

RECORDING AND RELEASE

As always in his pre-endorsement days, Slash used a Gibson Les Paul copy on the songs from *Appetite For Destruction*, with the distortion coming from a Marshall amp. For the clean parts of 'Sweet Child O' Mine' he used a Roland 120 Jazz Chorus amp that was lurking around the studio. Of the solo, a long, slow affair on which he gains the maximum expression from his Les Paul, he said: 'The saving grace for me was the solo section. That was a very organic solo that

came together simply, when we said, "Here's the chord change". It occurred very spontaneously, and I always looked forward to that part of the song in the set. It was completely different to the rest of the song.'

MUSICAL LEGACY

'Sweet Child O' Mine' may be a ballad, but it is also this resolutely hard-rocking band's signature song. It doesn't fit into any category, being too genuine in its sentiment to be a real wedding/funeral song, and too mellow to qualify as hard rock. Slash himself found it an irritant, saying: 'One of the things that always bugged me about "Sweet Child ..." was that it was an up-tempo ballad, which didn't fit what Guns N' Roses was all about, so that song annoyed me every time it came up in the set.' Not only that, the tricksy, string-skipping riff used to be too difficult to play when he'd had a few drinks, as was his wont. 'It really disturbed my drinking,' Slash added, 'because whenever we did a show I'd have a fair amount of whisky beforehand.' Fortunately, when he performed it (now sober full time) at the 2010 Superbowl – some say to the largest ever TV audience for the event – he nailed it.

GENRES

Hard rock

RECORDED

1986 in Los Angeles

PRODUCER

Mike Clink

BAND MEMBERS

Axl Rose, Slash, Izzy Stradlin, Duff McKagan, Steven Adler

http://flametr.com/sweet-child

Scan to see a video on your smartphone (incl. iPhone & Android)

GUNS N' ROSES

PARADISE CITY

When Tom Cruise sings your song, you know it's made an impression. The fun-sized movie star may not have broken box-office records when he sang Guns N' Roses' 'Paradise City' in the 2012 film *Rock Of Ages*, but then he didn't need to. The song has been imprinted on rock fans' DNA since its release in January 1989. Perhaps it was the song's nostalgia, or possibly it was that down-home arpeggiated intro which did it, but in all likelihood the popularity of 'Paradise City' comes from that exquisitely hummable chorus. Trivia fans will be delighted to learn that the original version of 'Take me down to the paradise city / Where the grass is green and the girls are pretty' was originally rendered as 'Take me down to the paradise city / Where the girls are fat and they've got big titties'. Truly, Guns N' Roses were silver-tongued poets of Wildean proportions.

RECORDING AND RELEASE

The amazing riff that begins after singer Axl Rose's blown whistle is essential Guns N' Roses, based on three ascending chromatic notes. Slash's riff, a little finger-twister, gets its solidity from Duff McKagan's scooped bass, played in tight unison. Slash's tone, a crunch straight from the drawer marked Aerosmith, was, he said in his 2008 autobiography, impossible to emulate after the fact, although he changed his tune when a signature amplifier was released some years later. Producer and engineer Mike Clink ensured that Slash's famed dexterity throughout the song – both in the riff and solo sections, and especially in the double-time ending – was rewarded by a silky guitar sound that had plenty of warmth. When 'Paradise City' was released on three vinyl formats plus cassette and CD, it was accompanied by a video clip in which Guns N' Roses are seen leaving a New York stadium in order to board a Concorde taking them to

the UK's Donington festival in 1988, cleverly disguising the fact that the band members were completely broke at the time. Fans bought into the image and made the song a huge hit.

MUSICAL LEGACY

It's amusing to note the spirit behind the many cover versions of 'Paradise City' that have emerged over the years. Hole, the grunge band fronted by Kurt Cobain's widow Courtney Love, played a version, presumably as an ironic gesture towards the mutual antipathy between Cobain and Axl Rose that had surfaced in the early 1990s. Then again, Warrior Soul did a respectful cover, giving it a tripped-out sheen, and Slash and Duff's later band Velvet Revolver gave it a going-over that was faithful to the original, as you might expect. Nowadays the glam-metal era is so far behind us that efforts such as the aforementioned Tom Cruise movie to give it some currency can only be seen as exercises in nostalgia. Nonetheless, when you strip all that away, you're still left with an amazing song, based on guitar work that is second to none.

GENRES

Hard rock, heavy metal

RECORDED

1986 in Los Angeles

PRODUCER

Mike Clink

BAND MEMBERS

Axl Rose, Slash, Izzy Stradlin, Duff McKagan, Steven Adler

THE JIMI HENDRIX EXPERIENCE

PURPLE HAZE

In March 1967 Jimi Hendrix had everything to prove. He'd landed smack in the middle of London's burgeoning psychedelic rock scene only six months previously and, while contemporaries such as Pete Townshend and Eric Clapton were awe-struck by his amazing abilities as a guitarist, the wider world had yet to hear many of his songs. 'Hey Joe' had set the pace in late 1966, but it was 'Purple Haze', the second single, that set the rock scene on fire, thanks to its perceived drug references (very much the order of the day in '67) and Hendrix's marvellous guitar manipulation. Anyone who saw him play this or any other song in his tragically brief career (he was jamming away in the sky by the autumn of 1970) is fortunate indeed.

RECORDING AND RELEASE

Central to the all-round amazingness of 'Purple Haze' is an E7♯9 chord, made so famous by our Jimi that pundits even refer to it as 'the Hendrix chord' to this day. Play it with open bottom E string, A string 7th fret, D string 6th fret, G string 7th fret, B string 8th fret and muted top E and you'll see why Paul McCartney, who had used the chord on 'Taxman' and other Beatles songs, referred to it as 'a great ham-fisted jazz chord'. However, Paul would have been more accurate if he'd labelled it a blues chord, containing as it does a nice, stressed-out clutch of mutually dissonant notes from the blues scale. It's this dissonance that gives the chord, and the all-time classic riff of which it is a part, its falling-apart, funky quality, and in turn this feeling gives 'Purple Haze' a genuine sense of danger. No wonder crowds and critics loved the song on its release, and that's before we even get to the solo, a thing of wonder played with the assistance of an octave pedal called the Octavia, built by British engineer Roger Mayer.

MUSICAL LEGACY

Before we even get to the multitude of musicians who have recorded 'Purple Haze', take a second to consider the impact of the title itself. Implying a psychedelic fuzz or state of bliss not unlike that induced by certain drugs, it has been used to evoke the idea of a spaced-out frame of mind in many a song, book, album and TV show title. There's a 2004 album of the same name by hip-hop artist Cam'ron, a 1982 film about a rebellious teen who is sent to fight in Vietnam, a strain of cannabis named after the song for its colour and potency, an American beer brand, an *a cappella* group ... everybody knows the name, if not its original source. As for cover versions, you can listen to Winger, Ozzy Osbourne, the Kronos Quartet, Tangerine Dream, The Cure, Buena Vista Social Club, Tommy Emmanuel and stacks of other musos for your fix of 'Purple Haze'. Even the youthful Brian May, in his pre-Queen band 1984, covered the song a few months after its original 1967 release.

GENRES

Psychedelic rock, acid rock, heavy metal

RECORDED

1967 in London

PRODUCER

Chas Chandler

BAND MEMBERS

Jimi Hendrix, Noel Redding, Mitch Mitchell

ON YOUTUBE  http://flametr.com/purple-hendrix

Scan to see a video on your smartphone (incl. iPhone & Android)

THE JIMI HENDRIX EXPERIENCE

FOXY LADY

1967 was the year in which The Jimi Hendrix Experience first stamped their mark on the international music scene, winding up the year with the excellent 'Foxy Lady', spelled 'Foxey Lady' on American versions of the *Are You Experienced?* album and still referred to that way Stateside. While the song was interpreted by many listeners as a simple expression of appreciation for a female of Hendrix's acquaintance, the singer later explained that when he addressed the fairer sex he was a little more subtle in his choice of words. The heavy-but-smooth riff at the core of the song was a root-plus-octave alternation, after which Hendrix overlaid upper-register fills and, like so much of his 1967–68 material, the song was upbeat and danceable while exuding the unmistakable patchouli scent of the Summer Of Love.

RECORDING AND RELEASE

Both in the studio and on stage, Hendrix played the main riff with help from his fretting-hand thumb, which he used to hold down the F♯ while switching between the root and its octave. Although live versions of 'Foxy Lady' are the ones to go for if you want to hear Hendrix extend it into a full-blown jam and play to the limit of his considerable abilities, the studio version helmed by Chas Chandler is still an anarchic affair by 1967 standards. Listen out for the sharp-edged riffs and feedback which Hendrix barely controls. On the live stage, of course, he would let the feedback ring out and shape it to assist with the solos. Once again, he used the 'Hendrix chord' that had first been heard in 'Purple Haze', released earlier that year. Mashed up with his big hands and overdriven through his Marshall amplifiers, the chord sounded not so much bluesy as threatening. Whoever the object of Hendrix's affection was in this song, she was in for quite a ride.

MUSICAL LEGACY

The years have not been kind to the word 'foxy' as an adjective; it's just too silly, too dated and too *Austin Powers* to take seriously. That said, the word and the song itself work perfectly in many situations, some comedic, some not. Take a look at the immortal 1992 comedy *Wayne's World*, in which perennial loser Garth sings the song while hip-thrusting his way towards the girl of his dreams ... in a dream. The host of musicians who have recorded a version of 'Foxy Lady' is impressive, however – even if they didn't mean it sincerely. The Red Hot Chili Peppers did a funked-up version, alongside Hendrix's 'Fire'. So did the venerable ZZ Top, one of the few bands in this book who were already a playing unit when Hendrix came to prominence. Lenny Kravitz also recorded a cover, unsurprisingly given his obvious Hendrix influence. Most prominently, Led Zeppelin guitarist Jimmy Page used to run through the song during one of his band's elephantine jams, especially during the epic 'Dazed And Confused'. That's quite an impact for a song about a pretty lady. Then again, what else is rock'n'roll really about?

GENRES

Rock, psychedelic rock

RECORDED

1966 in London

PRODUCER

Chas Chandler

BAND MEMBERS

Jimi Hendrix, Noel Redding, Mitch Mitchell

ON YOUTUBE http://flametr.com/foxy-hendrix

Scan to see a video on your smartphone (incl. iPhone & Android)

THE JIMI HENDRIX EXPERIENCE

VOODOO CHILD (SLIGHT RETURN)

The wah-wah pedal was a relatively new invention in 1970, when Jimi Hendrix used it to devastating effect on the unforgettable introduction of 'Voodoo Child (Slight Return)', not to be confused with 'Voodoo Chile', a much longer and more free-form blues workout played alongside the great Steve Winwood. Both songs are found on *Electric Ladyland*, the third and final album recorded by The Jimi Hendrix Experience. Indeed, '... Child' was based on '... Chile', as a shorter, more succinct song that grew from the original, with the addition of several key parts such as the heavily wah-wah'ed introduction that everyone, repeat everyone, knows. Just to add to the complexities, '... Child' was actually released under the title '... Chile' as a single, without the distinguishing '(Slight Return)'. Then, of course, there are people who pronounce 'Chile' like the South American country. As Jimi himself said, was this love or just confusion?

RECORDING AND RELEASE

The introduction is obviously the piece of guitar music which most rock fans know best, but in the case of 'Voodoo Child (Slight Return)' it's impossible to single out any part of the song – because Hendrix treats the entire composition as a vehicle for expression. He alternates between rhythm and lead playing in the blink of an eye, and both riffs and solos frequently pan from left to right to add to the swaying, hypnotic nature of the performance. His guitar parts are backed up by the solid, unwavering playing of bassist Noel Redding and drummer Mitch Mitchell, who allow him the breathing space he needs to take the dynamics down and up, via a slippery funk section that maximizes picking economy, to the fully expressive, dive-bombing pentatonics for which the song is justly famous.

Released in format somewhere between a single and an EP – 'Voodoo Child (Slight Return)' was backed with 'Hey Joe' and 'All Along The Watchtower', making up a mini Hendrix best-of of its own – the song continued to establish Hendrix's reputation as a man for whom a guitar was not simply an instrument. It was a vehicle for the expression of his soul.

MUSICAL LEGACY

Which legendary guitarist *hasn't* played part of this song at some point or other in their career? It seems that if you have the skills to operate a wah-wah pedal and a taste for classic rock, it's a mandatory part of your repertoire. The song has been hailed as an all-time classic by guitar wizard Joe Satriani among many others, who praised it as the very peak of guitar creativity. It has been covered by guitar players as varied as Yngwie Malmsteen, Stevie Ray Vaughan and Mick Mars of Mötley Crüe. Other bands who have taken a shot at the track include Extreme, Pearl Jam and Pride And Glory, the last of which featured Hendrix devotee Zakk Wylde. Who can say if the song would have been quite as successful if the wah-wah pedal hadn't been invented just in time for Jimi to use it?

GENRES

Acid rock, blues rock

RECORDED

1968 in New York

PRODUCER

Jimi Hendrix

BAND MEMBERS

Jimi Hendrix, Noel Redding, Mitch Mitchell

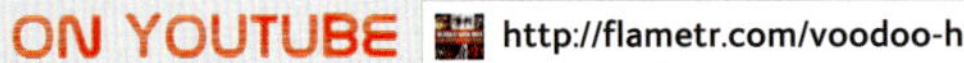

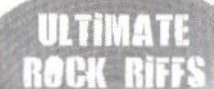

IRON BUTTERFLY

IN-A-GADDA-DA-VIDA

When Iron Butterfly released 'In-A-Gadda-Da-Vida' as an album track on the LP of the same name in 1968, many listeners scratched their heads. Was this a song? It lasted 17 minutes, for heaven's sake, and took up the whole of the album's flip side. A little later, the song was edited down to under three minutes – thus satisfying commercial radio stations' criteria for airplay – and people began to understand what the fuss was about. 'In-A-Gadda-Da-Vida' – which had started life as 'In The Garden of Eden' until an amusingly slurred version of that title stuck – was based on a solid riff that went on for six minutes in its original version, barely hindered by vocals. Focusing on a guitar and bass unison pattern that wormed its way into the listener's cerebral cortex until it stayed permanently, the group inadvertently created something of a minor heavy rock classic. They also became embroiled in the 'Who was the first heavy metal band?' debate that still rages to this day among people who think that they, or another of the 1960s' rock heavyweights, effectively started the movement.

RECORDING AND RELEASE

'In-A-Gadda-Da-Vida' is one of the few entries in the rock canon that was basically recorded unintentionally. When Iron Butterfly entered Ultrasonic Studios in Long Island and sound-checked for the studio engineer, Don Casale, they jammed the song in order for him to confirm that the instruments were balanced and in tune. Casale recorded the sound-check, and when the group listened back to the recording, they decided that it was good enough to use on the final album. Played live, the song would often come close to 20 minutes, as on the live LP which Iron Butterfly released in 1969. The group had always intended to insert solos into the song, they later explained, and took full

advantage of the opportunity to do so when playing 'In-A-Gadda-Da-Vida' live. It became one of the late 1960s' great jamming songs, perfectly evoking the spirit of the age.

MUSICAL LEGACY

'In-A-Gadda-Da-Vida' has been used in a multitude of TV shows and films, from *The Simpsons* to *The A Team* and beyond, and also spawned a few notable covers, although the song might not initially be thought of as an obvious candidate for a cover version. One came from the 1970s disco act Boney M, whose version exchanged the garage-level grime of the original for a polished sheen that worked surprisingly effectively. After all, what is disco music but a repeated figure that invites the listener to shake their booty? Another, diametrically opposed, version came in 1988 when Californian thrash metal band Slayer covered 'In-A-Gadda-Da-Vida' as the B-side of their song 'Mandatory Suicide'. In a sense the Boney M cover was the more successful. While the disco make-over gave 'In-A-Gadda-Da-Vida' a completely different spin, Slayer's take on the song was not radically altered from the original. and thus less interesting. The original remains a mesmerizing experience for anyone interested in the roots of heavy music.

GENRES

Acid rock, psychedelic rock, heavy metal

RECORDED

1968 in Long Island, New York

PRODUCER

Jim Hilton

BAND MEMBERS

Doug Ingle, Erik Brann, Lee Dorman, Ron Bushy

ON YOUTUBE  http://flametr.com/in-a-gadda

Scan to see a video on your smartphone (incl. iPhone & Android)

Coca-Cola

IRON MAIDEN

RUN TO THE HILLS

Riffs? Iron Maiden had 'em aplenty, and still do today, although few observers would deny that Maiden's golden era, which had begun in around 1980, was over by about 1988. The 1982 single 'Run To The Hills' was a glorious affair, bursting at the seams with optimism and aggressive energy. The London quintet were still relishing the speed of their emergence from the so-called 'New Wave Of British Heavy Metal', a club-sized scene from which the next obvious step led to the high-profile tours in stadiums which they continue to execute today. The wailing opening riff leads into the trademark Maiden gallop and onward through a splendid tale of white conquistadores invading America, with a balanced view of the conflict provided by a verse sung from the native Americans' viewpoint. Since the 1980s the song has been covered by many different musicians, from reality-TV show winners to lounge artists, and indeed Maiden have released several different remixed and live versions themselves. A 2002 version was issued in order to raise money for original drummer Clive Burr, now suffering from multiple sclerosis.

GENRES

Heavy metal

RECORDED

1982 in London

PRODUCER

Martin Birch

BAND MEMBERS

Bruce Dickinson, Dave Murray, Adrian Smith, Steve Harris, Clive Burr

http://flametr.com/run-to-the-hills

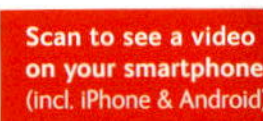

TAMA

IRON MAIDEN

THE TROOPER

British bands have never been too keen on proclaiming their Britishness, such a boast having often been viewed as jingoistic or worse, but Iron Maiden have never felt any qualms on the subject. 'The Trooper' tells of the military struggles endured by a soldier at the Battle Of Balaclava in 1854 and specifically the doom of the Light Brigade. Maiden singer Bruce Dickinson usually waves a Union Jack during the song and dons a redcoat uniform to underline the song's theme when singing it live, an exercise that audiences love. The snaky riff that begins the song is not for the faint-hearted (your fingers will fall off unless you're extremely talented), but is immediately recognizable to Maiden's legions of fans for that very reason. Later in the song, a stop-start riff has audiences on the edges of their seats for the full duration. It's that good, and it has been covered by a whole host of other metal bands both live and on record, notably by the Florida metal-core quartet Trivium.

GENRES

Heavy metal

RECORDED

1983 in Nassau, The Bahamas

PRODUCER

Martin Birch

BAND MEMBERS

Bruce Dickinson, Dave Murray, Adrian Smith, Steve Harris, Nicko McBrain

ON YOUTUBE  http://flametr.com/the-trooper-iron

MICHAEL JACKSON

BEAT IT

Michael Jackson's *Thriller* album was, like Prince's *Purple Rain* a couple of years later, the perfect synthesis of black soul and white rock, and sold in enormous quantities to all audiences for decades after its release as a result. A highlight of the album was 'Beat It', which sucked listeners in with its apocalyptic, synthesized intro, its hypnotic beat and the phenomenal, tapped solo delivered on its mid-section by guest musician Eddie Van Halen. That solo, a simplified version of the extremely complex solos which Van Halen routinely laid down with his band, had to be tamed by producer Quincy Jones before the final mix. Jones thought that the original high-gain distortion would be too much for audiences and radio programmers, and gave it a smoother sound. Eddie Van Halen later recalled that he did the solo as a favour to Jackson and Jones, without asking for a fee – a move that he said made the rest of Van Halen look on him as a fool. If only he'd asked for 10 percent of the royalties.

GENRES

Rock, hard rock

RECORDED

1982 in Los Angeles

PRODUCER

Quincy Jones

BAND MEMBERS

Michael Jackson, Paul Jackson, Jr, Steve Lukather, Eddie Van Halen, Steve Porcaro, Greg Phillinganes, Bill Wolfer, Tom Bahler, Jeff Porcaro

JUDAS PRIEST

BREAKING THE LAW

'We were the first British heavy metal band,' said Judas Priest singer Rob Halford in the early 2000s, with good reason. While acknowledging the role played by Black Sabbath, whose debut album came four years before Priest's, Halford pointed out that blues-rock formed a significant element in Sabbath's sound, therefore Priest, who never really dabbled in a blues sound, were the first out of the metallic blocks. All of which posturing is amusing in hindsight, now that death metal, black metal and grindcore, three of the most bludgeoning genres of music ever invented, are commonplace. The best-known singles by Priest, of which 'Breaking The Law' is definitely one, pale in comparison, and yet, at the time of their release, they seemed genuinely threatening. Although perhaps less so when you watched the video.

RECORDING AND RELEASE

For Judas Priest's 1980 album *British Steel*, the Midlands quintet were considering a change in their sound, and wrote shorter, more easily digestible songs. 'Breaking The Law' is more of a hard rock song than a metal tune as a result, with a simple, hummable melody, a more modern guitar sound than Priest's previous work and a repeated chorus that begged audiences to punch the air.

The video, you say? Pure kitsch. Directed by Sex Pistols biopic maker Julien Temple, the clip depicted Judas Priest travelling by car on the decidedly un-rock'n'roll route of the A406 in North London. Entering a bank, Halford plus heavily disguised guitarists K.K. Downing and Glen Tipton hold up the staff, but not with guns – with guitars! Rather than chuckling and going about their business, the staff hand over a gold disc, which the band grab before

embarking on the return journey down the North Circular. In some ways it's quite brilliant. Audiences certainly thought so, making the single a huge hit and imploring for the song to be played every time Judas Priest play.

MUSICAL LEGACY

'Breaking The Law', like the rest of the tracks on the *British Steel* album, is regarded as a stone-cold, classic heavy metal song. The album enjoyed its 30th anniversary back in 2010 and a host of musicians were asked for their thoughts on it. What was interesting was that a large number of American musicians in their forties viewed it as absolutely essential to their development as metallers. While Priest's heyday in their home country was over by the early 1980s, when fashions dictated that they embark on a series of experiments with keyboards and other modern fripperies, in America the fan base stayed loyal despite these strategic errors. After Priest spent much of the 1990s without singer Halford, struggling to retain a toehold as a result, the classic line-up re-formed and found immense acclaim waiting for them. Ten years later, Priest are enjoying the kind of respect previously afforded to acts such as Sabbath and even Led Zeppelin. Songs like 'Breaking The Law' are directly responsible for this.

GENRES

Heavy metal, hard rock

RECORDED

1980 in Ascot, Berkshire

PRODUCER

Tom Allom

BAND MEMBERS

Rob Halford, K.K. Downing, Glen Tipton, Ian Hill, Dave Holland

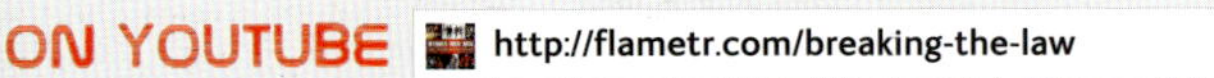

JUDAS PRIEST

ELECTRIC EYE

All the best heavy metal is based on fantasy literature and, in July 1982, Judas Priest hit the bullseye with 'Electric Eye', taken from their *Screaming For Vengeance* album and clearly inspired by George Orwell's *1984*. As that year approached and headlines talked of the Cold War, Ronald Reagan's Star Wars programme and the rise of CCTV surveillance, Priest turned this general paranoia into a song based on a mighty opening riff. This nifty, even catchy little pattern appears both on the album and in live shows after an instrumental introduction called 'The Hellion' and serves to whip audiences into a metallic lather. Recognizing the song's classic status in metal history, bands such as Helloween, As I Lay Dying and even nu-metal miserablists Godsmack have covered it over the years. But there's something about the original Priest version that makes it the most convincing. Driven, uncompromising and more than a little bit camp, it's one of the 1980s' most recognizable heavy tunes. A recent 30th anniversary reissue of *Screaming For Vengeance* was a reminder of how epic Priest were way back when.

GENRES

Heavy metal

RECORDED

1982 in Ibiza, Spain

PRODUCER

Tom Allom

BAND MEMBERS

Rob Halford, K.K. Downing, Glen Tipton, Ian Hill, Dave Holland

Scan to see a video on your smartphone (incl. iPhone & Android)

THE KILLERS

MR BRIGHTSIDE

Released in May 2004, 'Mr Brightside' was a huge hit in many countries for several reasons. It was as catchy as hell thanks to the dinky high-register riff that began it and was soon joined by a thumping, descending bass part. Secondly, it contained a synth wash, which in these post-modern, Eighties-worshipping times is always a good thing. What's more, the song was supposedly based on singer Brandon Flowers' feelings of intense jealousy regarding an unidentified ex-lover, and who can't identify with that? Finally, the song contained lyrics about a woman removing her dress, again an effective selling point. But it's that riff to which the listener's brain returns, time and time again. It didn't take long for 'Mr Brightside' to become ubiquitous. The Killers sang it in the cult teen TV series *The OC* to great effect and the song hit big in the UK thanks to a popular cover by the fluffy rock quartet McFly. For a while back in 2004 and 2005, 'Mr Brightside' was impossible to avoid, although as with all pop music, the glitter eventually faded.

GENRES

Post-punk revival, new wave, indie rock

RECORDED

2001 in Henderson, Nevada; 2003 in Berkeley, California

PRODUCER

The Killers

BAND MEMBERS

Brandon Flowers, Dave Keuning, Mark Stoermer, Ronnie Vannucci

http://flametr.com/mr-brightside

THE KINKS

YOU REALLY GOT ME

Oh, to be a part of the music business in London in 1964. Times were a-changing, rapidly and permanently. Rhythm and blues was all the rage (the original R&B, not your modern dishwater) and the scene's 'faces' were waiting for it to morph into the new sound of mod. In amongst all this were The Kinks, whose tender years belied their excellent grasp of the blues idiom and whose innate inventiveness was quickly gaining them a fan base. Proof of this inventive streak came when guitarist Dave Davies, brother of singer Ray, cut a hole in the speaker cone of his Elpico amplifier with a razor blade and poked holes in it with a pin. This created a trebly fuzz tone, an invaluable asset in the days before distortion pedals were commonly available. With this new sound, the band were able to play taut, riff-based pop songs that sounded like a keen new innovation to the blues-obsessed music fans of the day.

RECORDING AND RELEASE

Rumours have abounded for close to 40 years that the guitar solo – which, it has to be said, is a fairly rudimentary blues affair – was played by session legend and soon to be Led Zeppelin founder Jimmy Page. He has denied it. Producer Shel Talmy denied it too, although he did state that Page played rhythm guitar with The Kinks on at least one occasion. It has been claimed that the somewhat snooty blues community of the day resented the sudden success of The Kinks, a bunch of teenagers whose taste in clothing surpassed their musical ability in some naysayers' eyes, and thus the rumour was deliberately begun in order to discredit the band. Another juicy nugget from the recording of this iconic song is that it contains the words 'f*** off', spoken in at least partial jest by Dave Davies

in response to his brother Ray's exhortations to get in the mood before playing the solo. According to Ray Davies, the words are clearly audible during the drum break that precedes the solo. He added that with the emergence of digital re-mastering, the retort in question is ever more obvious to the listener.

MUSICAL LEGACY

Many critics, music historians and other professional commentators have stated that the overdriven guitar sound on 'You Really Got Me' marked the birth of heavy metal. This is wrong. The truth is that the overdriven guitar sound marked the birth of overdriven guitar sounds. The Kinks were not a metal band. They were a supremely arch, knowing bunch of aesthetes whose grasp of a sardonic lyric and a sharp suit was second only to The Who, whose guitarist Pete Townshend admitted that his early song 'I Can't Explain' was written in homage to 'You Really Got Me' (but without the slashed speakers; The Who just smashed the amps up instead).

GENRES

Hard rock, garage rock

RECORDED

1964 in London

PRODUCER

Shel Talmy

BAND MEMBERS

Ray Davies, Dave Davies, Pete Quaife, Bobby Graham, Arthur Greenslade, Mick Avory

ON YOUTUBE  http://flametr.com/really-got-me

THE KINKS

ALL DAY AND ALL OF THE NIGHT

Released in October 1964, just two months after 'You Really Got Me', The Kinks' equally well-known hit 'All Day And All Of The Night' sounded like its predecessor in more ways than one. Dave Davies's raw, overdriven guitar sound – the result of a deliberately mutilated speaker cone in his amplifier – was in place for the fantastic riff that opens and sustains the song, and over which his brother Ray's vocal melody lies in unison. The sexual implications of the lyrics in both songs are evident, with 'You Really Got Me' easily interpreted as 'You've Certainly Stirred Up My Loins, Madam' and 'All Day And All Of The Night' clearly meaning ... well, you can probably figure that out for yourself. Both songs have been covered endlessly in intervening decades, with the most successful version of 'All Day ...' coming from progressive punks The Stranglers in 1988. Like the original version, the guitar solo was a thing of pure sonic weakness, but the riffs were extremely solid. Proof that rhythm guitar is where it's at, daddio.

GENRES

Hard rock, garage rock, protopunk

RECORDED

1964 in London

PRODUCER

Shel Talmy

BAND MEMBERS

Ray Davies, Dave Davies, Pete Quaife, Mick Avory

ON YOUTUBE  http://flametr.com/all-day-kinks

Scan to see a video on your smartphone (incl. iPhone & Android)

Ludwig
The
KINKS

LENNY KRAVITZ

ARE YOU GONNA GO MY WAY

Traditional hard rock was, to coin a phrase, in a hard place in 1993, with grunge and the burgeoning alt-rock scenes occupying MTV viewers' attention. However, that failed to trouble axe-slinger Lenny Kravitz, who dished up this splendid bit of commercial riffery and watched it assault the charts in dozens of countries. The opening riff, a descending figure plus tail, was a stroke of genius, propelling the song forward into one of the hypnotic grooves that Kravitz had been peddling to good effect since his emergence at the end of the 1980s. Note his keen awareness of song dynamics: the riff stops and starts repeatedly throughout 'Are You Gonna Go My Way', giving audiences what they wanted and also the chance for our man and his second guitarist Craig Ross (who counterpoints the main riff with a higher-register figure) to do a bit of crowd-pleasing showboating. Tom Jones covered the song on his *Reload* album in 1999, ably assisted by the then young whippersnapper Robbie Williams, giving the tune a new lease of life to UK crowds.

GENRES

Hard rock, funk rock, psychedelic rock

RECORDED

1992–93 in Hoboken, New Jersey

PRODUCER

Lenny Kravitz

BAND MEMBERS

Lenny Kravitz, Craig Ross, Tony Breit, Cindy Blackman

ON YOUTUBE  http://flametr.com/gonna-go

LED ZEPPELIN

HEARTBREAKER

All these years since Led Zeppelin decided to cease activities in the wake of their drummer John Bonham's death from alcohol-induced asphyxiation, some of their millions of fans may have forgotten what an extraordinary amount of activity the group squeezed into a few short years. Zep's second album, *II*, appeared just nine months after their debut LP, but it contained a stack of all-time classic rock tunes that still endure four decades and more later. Jimmy Page, who had spent years as a session man extraordinaire in London before graduating to the Yardbirds and then to his own band, was the riffmaster general, knocking out endless guitar lines of world-class quality. Recording that many sessions will do that to your guitar technique, and in Page's case all those days, weeks and years spent in damp recording studios had obviously lent him a keen understanding of the power of the almighty *ostinato*.

RECORDING AND RELEASE

One of the great things about that maddeningly catchy riff is that some people, even the professionals, seem to think that Led Zeppelin messed it right up, although with a bit of thought it's evident that they did no such thing. 'It's one of the greatest riffs in rock,' commented super-producer Rick Rubin about 'Heartbreaker', adding, 'It starts and it's like they don't really know where the "one" is [the first beat of the bar]. Magical in its awkwardness.' Rubin wasn't quite right here. When Page plays the riff, he deliberately starts on the fourth beat of the bar, which is hardly inadvertent or an error, it is done to provide a lead-up, as it were, to the first beat of the riff. After this, the song becomes an awe-inspiring lesson in guitar fluency and inventiveness, with the different sections of the song ebbing

and flowing. In line with Zeppelin's no-singles policy – they only ever wanted to be taken seriously as an albums band – 'Heartbreaker' was released as part of the mothership LP, on which it remains a high point.

MUSICAL LEGACY

Live, 'Heartbreaker' was a fan favourite from the very beginning. Page would extend it, as was his perennial wont, improvising his solo and adding bits of Bach and even Simon & Garfunkel, with Zep's rhythm section of John Paul Jones and John Bonham anchoring his experiments with panache. Part of a live version from Madison Square Gardens in New York appears in the 1976 film *The Song Remains The Same*, but the whole didn't appear until the accompanying album was re-mastered in 2007. Of the occasional cover versions that have cropped up since, Nirvana's is the most notable, with a live version included on their *With The Lights Out* box set in 2004. Nick Hornby also wrote about the song in his 2002 essay book *31 Songs*, in which he explained the special resonance that 'Heartbreaker' had for him, a resonance that is still shared by a generation of thinking rock fans.

GENRES

Hard rock, heavy metal, blues rock

RECORDED

1969 in New York

PRODUCER

Jimmy Page

BAND MEMBERS

Robert Plant, Jimmy Page, John Paul Jones, John Bonham

ON YOUTUBE  http://flametr.com/heartbreaker-led

LED ZEPPELIN

WHOLE LOTTA LOVE

It's interesting to note that the immortal 'Whole Lotta Love', released in November 1969, has equal if not greater significance for a generation of now middle-aged people who were mere toddlers when it first appeared. This is the case because, for many years, the song was the title song of the BBC's music flagship, *Top Of The Pops*. Many a 1980s kid will recall the sounds of Zeppelin, incongruously in retrospect, signalling the beginning of what was essentially the only way to keep up with the mid-Eighties New Romantic scene on TV. In choosing the Zep tune to head up its Thursday night prime-time viewing, the Beeb gave 'Whole Lotta Love' back the excitement that had accompanied it back in 1969, when men were men and the entire concept of Duran Duran and Spandau Ballet would have caused grown-ups to faint.

RECORDING AND RELEASE

Released as a single in several territories outside the UK – at home Led Zep's and manager Peter Grant's no-singles edict held firm – 'Whole Lotta Love' was a huge hit, with that stuttering rhythm and suggestive lyric grabbing the imagination of entire nations. While Page's riff was an original, singer Robert Plant later admitted to *Uncut* magazine that he had 'borrowed' some of the vocal phrasing from Willie Dixon, the blues singer, who had previously written a song called 'You Need Love'. A lawsuit came about in 1985 and Zeppelin lost. As Plant is reported to have explained, 'Page's riff was Page's riff. It was there before anything else. I just thought, "Well, what am I going to sing?" That was it, a nick. Now happily paid for. At the time, there was a lot of conversation about what to do. It was decided that it was so far away in time and influence that ... well, you only get caught when you're successful. That's the game.'

Admirable though Plant's honesty was, it is a little difficult to understand how a band of such stature and talent would resort to using someone else's musical ideas. But as Plant said, that's the game.

MUSICAL LEGACY

'Whole Lotta Love', Zep's only Top 10 single in America, was often chosen to close their live sets. As was so often the case with Zeppelin's bluesier material, the band dragged the song out into a wild and wonderful cornucopia of jams, including sections from other songs such as 'Your Time Is Gonna Come', 'Good Times Bad Times' and 'The Lemon Song' within it. They also threw in segments of classic rock'n'roll songs by legends such as Eddie Cochran and Elvis Presley. The song was also destined to be the last that the original foursome would play, although after Bonham's death the three surviving members have regrouped to play it three times. The first occasion was Live Aid in 1985, the second came three years later at Atlantic Records' 40th Anniversary concert and the most recent to date has been the Ahmet Ertegun Tribute Concert at London's O_2 Arena in December 2007.

GENRES

Hard rock, blues rock, heavy metal

RECORDED

1969 in New York and Los Angeles

PRODUCER

Jimmy Page

BAND MEMBERS

Robert Plant, Jimmy Page, John Paul Jones, John Bonham

ON YOUTUBE  http://flametr.com/whole-lotta-love

Scan to see a video on your smartphone (incl. iPhone & Android)

LED ZEPPELIN

BLACK DOG

By 1970, just a year or two into their incredible career, Led Zeppelin were already being acknowledged as one of the biggest rock bands ever formed – perhaps even *the* biggest. One of the side effects of being in a band this big and famous is that no end of lesser, copycat bands shoot up in your wake, nicking your sound and look, and passing you off as an influence. Zep had nabbed so many phrases and riffs from the blues canon that they could hardly complain when other bands started to sound more than a little 'Pagey and Planty', but nonetheless they decided to write a song in 1970 that your average bar band wouldn't be able to cover, because it was just too damn complicated. Thus was 'Black Dog' born, and to this day you will rarely hear it played down the Dog & Duck in the average commuter town because very few non-professional musicians can make head or tail of the key riff, the arrangement and the time signature, let alone replicate Robert Plant's helium-level vocals.

RECORDING AND RELEASE

The rich, shifting arrangement of 'Black Dog' is its greatest strength. It is one of Zeppelin's all-time career-best songs, standing as it does at the highpoint of *IV*, the album which many (but by no means all) fans regard as their most accomplished work. Laid down over a period of three or four months at Headley Grange in East Hampshire, England, 'Black Dog' moves from that complex riff, which moves back on itself over several different time signatures, to a call-and-response section alternating between Plant's *a cappella* vocal and the same, near-impossible-to-replicate riff. Drummer John Bonham can be heard between the riff sections, tapping his sticks together to indicate when the band should come in, a sound the band attempted to mute during production but which was impossible to mask

completely with 1970s studio technology. It's interesting to note that the sounds at the beginning of the song can be identified as Page warming up the 'army of guitars', as he referred to it, each riff triple-tracked for a full, wall of sound effect. 'Black Dog' was subsequently released as a single in several territories and went on to become one of the most recognizable songs from the entire Zeppelin canon.

MUSICAL LEGACY

'Black Dog' was debuted on stage in Belfast in 1971, and also appeared in Zeppelin's O_2 Arena show set list in 2007 – remarkable longevity for a song that was basically designed to deter people from trying to play it. Its legacy is not merely that of a decent song, it also proved that this group of blues lovers could compete in the musical stakes with the fleetest-fingered of their musical contemporaries. This was no mean claim in the era of progressive rock, when few musos understood the 'less is more' credo and were at pains to play as many notes as possible. In retrospect, you can see why punk had to happen.

GENRES

Hard rock

RECORDED

1970–71 in Headley Grange, East Hampshire

PRODUCER

Jimmy Page

BAND MEMBERS

Robert Plant, Jimmy Page, John Paul Jones, John Bonham

ON YOUTUBE  http://flametr.com/black-dog-led

LED ZEPPELIN

KASHMIR

By 1975 Led Zeppelin had reached the zenith of their considerable songwriting and arranging powers. 'Kashmir', a song that redefines the massively overused word 'epic', is based on an ascending riff played initially on guitars tuned to DADGAD, augmented later in its eight-minute duration by strings, brass and a Mellotron. John Bonham's mighty drums are given a phased sound through an Eventide unit, lending the song a spacey feel that is nonetheless firmly anchored to the ground. There is something about the ambition of 'Kashmir' and its stadium-sized dimensions that make it unique. Singer Robert Plant called it 'the pride of Led Zeppelin' and it became the most recognized song on its parent album, *Physical Graffiti*. It has transcended its genre through samples and other uses in pop and hip-hop, most notably a song called 'Come With Me' recorded in 1998 by Puff Daddy for the *Godzilla* soundtrack. In the whole of 1970s rock music, few songs have as much weight or as much continued relevance as 'Kashmir', simply because it sounds so huge.

GENRES

Hard rock

RECORDED

1974 in Headley, East Hampshire

PRODUCER

Jimmy Page

BAND MEMBERS

Robert Plant, Jimmy Page, John Paul Jones, John Bonham

ON YOUTUBE  http://flametr.com/kashmir-led

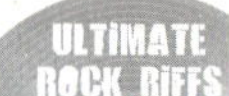

LYNYRD SKYNYRD

SWEET HOME ALABAMA

Even as late as 1974, according to many cultural observers, America was still in two halves. There was the affluent, sophisticated north and the redneck south, and never the twain would meet, they thought, although this black-and-white definition of the world's most powerful country, then as now, was far too simplistic to hold up under scrutiny. Still, when Florida country-rock group Lynyrd Skynyrd attempted to address the subject of Southern pride in their signature song 'Sweet Home Alabama', sensitivities to the issue were keen enough to set off a nationwide controversy. All because of a little ditty about a state, based on an infuriatingly catchy riff.

RECORDING AND RELEASE

Ed King was strumming a guitar at a Skynyrd practice one night when he heard the group's other guitarist, Gary Rossington, playing the line that was eventually used to counterpoint the famous verse riff in the song that became 'Sweet Home Alabama'. Intrigued, he, drummer Bob Burns and bassist Leon Wilkeson created the basic backing track and the song was born. Its lyrics were partially inspired by Neil Young's songs 'Southern Man' and 'Alabama', in which the Canadian singer-songwriter discussed recent racism in the Southern states, as well as the South's history of slavery. Inspired to point out that these social ills were confined to a mere minority in Alabama and elsewhere in the South, Skynyrd pushed 'Sweet Home Alabama' in a moderately political direction with its mention of the recent presidential election won by Jimmy Carter and also the pro-segregation Alabama Governor George Wallace. 'In Birmingham they love the governor,' went Ronnie Van Zant's lyric, followed by a series of boos that many listeners failed to hear or appreciate, thus leading some people to suppose that the song endorsed racism.

MUSICAL LEGACY

All these years later, times have changed and much of the sting – inasmuch as there was any outside critics' circles – has faded from 'Sweet Home Alabama'. Today the song is regarded within and outside America as a pretty harmless bit of nostalgic whimsy, but it casts a long musical shadow. The main riff was sampled by Kid Rock, a film bore the same title (and included the same cheesy themes) in 2002, and even Metallica indirectly used it when they wrote their 1983 song 'The Four Horsemen' (the band's then-member Dave Mustaine, later of Megadeth, played the famous descending chord sequence in the song's middle eight). Hip-hop fans will also recall that in the 2002 movie *8 Mile*, rapper Eminem improvised a routine over the song in a scene where it can be heard in the background. Substituting 'I'm living in a trailer' for the chorus, Eminem deftly mocks a great American institution, albeit affectionately; it's an interesting glimpse of the modern world meeting an outdated one. This is not meant to imply that 'Sweet Home Alabama' isn't a great song, because it is – but there is no doubt that the sun has long since set on the great country-rock scene of three decades (and more) ago.

GENRES

Southern rock, country rock

RECORDED

1973 in Doraville, Georgia

PRODUCER

Al Kooper

BAND MEMBERS

Ronnie Van Zant, Gary Rossington, Allen Collins, Ed King, Billy Powell, Leon Wilkeson, Bob Burns

ON YOUTUBE  http://flametr.com/sweet-home-alabama

MACHINE HEAD

DAVIDIAN

Along with Texan metallers Pantera, the Californian quartet Machine Head were in the process of redefining mainstream heavy metal in August 1994 when their debut album *Burn My Eyes* was released. Its high point was arguably 'Davidian', written in response to the Waco massacre of the previous year. A rich, groove-heavy amalgam of down-stroked, down-tuned power chords and pinch harmonics, the song was based on several immensely heavyweight riffs from start to finish. 'Davidian''s greatest punch to the gut comes after three and a half minutes, when a vast outro riff is introduced, lasting another minute and more and fading gradually. As singer and guitarist Robb Flynn has often explained, not least in the foreword to this very book, the best riffs are often the simplest ones, and there's nothing complex about the internal notes of this one. However, as an exercise in triple-picking and palm-muting, it has rarely been bettered. Talk about a way to end a song. All heavy metal songwriters should have this riff on permanent repeat if they want to make an impact.

GENRES

Heavy metal, groove metal

RECORDED

1994 in California

PRODUCER

Colin Richardson

BAND MEMBERS

Robb Flynn, Logan Mader, Adam Duce, Chris Kontos

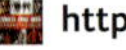
http://flametr.com/davidian-machine

Scan to see a video on your smartphone (incl. iPhone & Android)

MANIC STREET PREACHERS

MOTORCYCLE EMPTINESS

Conflating emo references with a classic rock guitar lick more befitting rock titans Journey, the Manic Street Preachers created a truly beautiful anthem for a generation with 'Motorcycle Emptiness'. Later Manic Street Preachers songs such as 'A Design For Life' and 'Everything Must Go' may have been equally anthemic, and 'The Intense Humming Of Evil' more apocalyptic, but the Manics never wrote a more heartstring-plucking song than this 1992 hit. Singer and guitarist James Dean Bradfield somehow hit upon a plangent, soaring tone with his Gibson Les Paul that doesn't overstay its welcome, complementing the much more subtle arpeggiated tones of the backing track. It's a curious amalgam of torch song and mosh-pit classic as a result, and is tinged with mystery to this day thanks to the continued absence of second guitarist and songwriter Richey Edwards, who went missing in 1995. His disappearance has sparked a long-lived collection of conspiracy theories and rumours. For many of the Manics' fans, the song stands as an epitaph to their fallen hero.

GENRES

Alternative rock, hard rock

RECORDED

1991 in Woking, Surrey

PRODUCER

Steve Brown

BAND MEMBERS

James Dean Bradfield, Richey Edwards, Nicky Wire, Sean Moore

http://flametr.com/motorcycle-manic

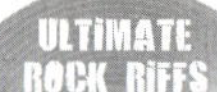

MEGADETH

SYMPHONY OF DESTRUCTION

Thrash metallers Megadeth were peaking commercially in 1992 with the *Countdown To Extinction* album, although they didn't know it. Like their old rivals Metallica, the band had smoothed down their sound, reducing tempos and buffing away the raw edges of their music to produce a slick, highly digestible form of heavy metal that sold in huge numbers. Witness the opening riff of the big hit, 'Symphony Of Destruction': a simple, crunching figure that focused on bandleader Dave Mustaine's expert down strokes and bassist David Ellefson's machine-like unison playing. As a lead guitarist, Mustaine is world famous, but 'Deth fans who also play guitar have known since the late 1980s that his rhythm chops are also insanely developed. Hear them in full effect on this song, which begins with a snatch of Mozart, just to show the world that metal musicians are cultured too. As for the lyrics, which muse on the subject of an unidentified human seizing control of the world via some form of totalitarian government, it's classic metal inspiration, as it should be.

GENRES

Heavy metal

RECORDED

1992 in Burbank, California

PRODUCER

Max Norman, Dave Mustaine

BAND MEMBERS

Dave Mustaine, Marty Friedman, David Ellefson, Nick Menza

 http://flametr.com/symphony-megadeth

Jackson

METALLICA

MASTER OF PUPPETS

As headbangers worldwide will tell you, the most accomplished thrash metal album ever recorded is either Slayer's *Reign In Blood* or Metallica's *Master Of Puppets*. *Puppets* is the more melodic, lacking the maddened nihilism of *Reign*, but replacing it with a sense of refined malevolence that peaks on the album's title track. Picking out a single riff from this complex song is not easy, as it contains several classic metal guitar patterns and switches rapidly and often between them. However, the second and third riffs, both spidery affairs played with millimetrically precise down strokes by rhythm guitar genius James Hetfield, continue to hold positions on most guitar teachers' most-requested riff lists. Play these with any accuracy – ideally while barking out lyrics about the command that evil drugs have over their users – and you're well on the way towards heavy metal mastery. The fact that Hetfield recorded this song and the other *Puppets* songs at the tender age of 22 still beggars belief, and that's not even including Metallica's previous album *Ride The Lightning*, itself an eye-wateringly tricky set of songs.

GENRES

Thrash metal

RECORDED

1985 in Copenhagen

PRODUCER

Flemming Rasmussen

BAND MEMBERS

James Hetfield, Kirk Hammett, Cliff Burton, Lars Ulrich

ON YOUTUBE  http://flametr.com/master-puppets

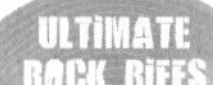

Marshall
AMPLIFICATION

METALLICA

ENTER SANDMAN

Metallica's fifth album, a self-titled affair that has gone on to sell over 20 million copies in the USA and several bazillion in the rest of the world, is such a massively iconic entity in heavy metal that it deserves to have its cover carved into a mountain, Mount Rushmore-style. Not that there's much of a cover: it's black with black lettering and a black snake etched onto it. None more black, as they say, and its starkness is highly representative of the band's ethos, which was a deliberate departure from the complex, even progressive thrash metal that had typified their previous album, 1988's ... *And Justice For All*. Simple, stripped-down grooves and riffs were the order of the day at Metallica's house, it seemed, and no riff came simpler or more stripped-down than the one that anchored the opening song, 'Enter Sandman'.

RECORDING AND RELEASE

Guitarist Kirk Hammett came up with the key riff, a simple, down-stroked E power chord and F hammer-on which featured a tail of G, E, F♯, E, F♯, G, F♯ and E. You might think such a simple riff would have already been done, and in fact some critics noted the similarity of its arpeggiated intro to a little-known song by a band called Excel, but Hammett's riff was original enough to be the foundation of the song. Struggling to find the right lyrics and uncertain if 'Enter Sandman' was the right single to lead off the *Metallica* campaign, singer James Hetfield was initially dubious about the song's potential, but, urged on by drummer Lars Ulrich, he relented and saw sense. The song was a huge hit and has gone on to top regular charts in magazines for 'Best Metal Song' and other page-filling exercises. To this day, no Metallica concert is complete without a rendition of this epic song, invariably with added pyrotechnics.

TAMA

MUSICAL LEGACY

Quite apart from its success as a song in its own right, 'Enter Sandman' helped Metallica to reshape heavy music in 1991, the Year Zero which wiped out 75 per cent of all heavy-metal bands with roots in the 1980s. From that year on, mainstream metal was about anthemic choruses rather than warp-speed thrash beats. Fans of Metallica's early, thrashier work were disappointed with their new sound, but millions of new fans came on board and the group's fan base quadrupled overnight. 'Enter Sandman' was also the first Metallica song to have a bottom-heavy production, to bassist Jason Newsted's particular delight. Producer Bob Rock, drafted in by Metallica to give them a commercial sound after his work with The Cult and Mötley Crüe, mixed Newsted's bass high, a complete change from the … *And Justice For All* mix, which featured almost no bass. In doing so, Rock gave Metallica's newly commercial music a sound that radio and MTV would buy into. And that, folks, is how Metallica became the biggest heavy metal band there has ever been or indeed will ever be.

GENRES

Heavy metal

RECORDED

1990–91 in Los Angeles

PRODUCER

Bob Rock

BAND MEMBERS

James Hetfield, Kirk Hammett, Jason Newsted, Lars Ulrich

ON YOUTUBE  http://flametr.com/enter-metallica

Scan to see a video on your smartphone (incl. iPhone & Android)

MÖTLEY CRÜE

DR FEELGOOD

Of the tidal wave of hairspray-laden glam-metal bands that poured out of Hollywood in the 1980s, the only groups to endure to the present day with the remotest shred of dignity are Guns N' Roses and Mötley Crüe. The latter, a slightly older band than Guns N' Roses, who had emerged onto the international scene a couple of years earlier, took the standard glam influences (New York Dolls, Aerosmith, Sex Pistols, Mick Ronson) and added their own edge to create the 1980s glam blueprint. Their best album is very probably *Dr Feelgood*, although fans will bicker about this for time immemorial, because it came out at glam's peak and because the songs – especially the title track – were highly infectious. 'Dr Feelgood' itself comes with a funky ascending riff played by guitarist Mick Mars with great dexterity, and is loaded with lyrics about a reliable chap who deals in high-quality substances. This debauched stuff sounded great in the years before grunge came along and rock became serious again, but never fear, Mötley Crüe returned to fight another day. They still play the world's biggest stadiums.

GENRES

Heavy metal, glam metal

RECORDED

1988 in Vancouver

PRODUCER

Bob Rock

BAND MEMBERS

Vince Neil, Mick Mars, Nikki Sixx, Tommy Lee

MOTÖRHEAD

ACE OF SPADES

Most bands who last four decades can only do so because they've made a comfortable wedge of cash. The idea of spending that long in a cramped tour bus with roadies leaving their socks around would be too much for most sane humans to take. That is not the case with Motörhead, however. Although their signature song, 'Ace Of Spades', was released way, way back in October 1980, the band never really made the money they deserved, as frontman and founder Ian 'Lemmy' Kilmister has always made clear. So they're still on the road all these years later, playing 'Ace Of Spades' and other, even older signature songs such as 'Overkill'. You can't tour that long and play the same old songs without getting mighty sick of them, and for Lemmy 'Ace Of Spades' lost its flavour decades ago. However, showman that he is, he insists that Motörhead will always play the song live. 'We can't ditch "Ace Of Spades", it wouldn't be right,' he once said. 'If I go to see Little Richard, I expect to hear "Good Golly Miss Molly", or I'd be p***ed off.'

RECORDING AND RELEASE

There are two essential riffs to this most essential of rock songs (whether 'Ace Of Spades' is rock or metal is a debate for another time; let's just say Lemmy favours rock). The first is the opening bass riff delivered by Lemmy himself, a simple two-note job plus upward slide. This ushers in 'Fast' Eddie Clarke's equally simple (but effective) riff, a meaty figure that returns in between Lemmy's ursine roar. The lyrics are perhaps Lemmy's most devastating yet, at least if themes of staying up late and indulging in banned substances are of interest to you. Using gambling analogies to describe Motörhead's relentless lifestyle, Lemmy throws in a 'And don't forget the joker!' after the line 'I don't wanna live forever', a typically no-nonsense retort to the idea of life, death and the way either should be executed.

MUSICAL LEGACY

There are very few more important songs in the entire catalogue of British heavy rock than 'Ace Of Spades'. It has been covered by innumerable heavy-metal bands, of course, but its real significance has come with its appearance in other areas of culture, from comedy through sports to video games. Who could forget Motörhead's appearance on *The Young Ones* in 1984? British readers over 35 will recall Lemmy leaning backwards to sing the song at a neck-breaking angle because the mic was so high, while the rest of the cast of the classic surrealist sitcom do their merry caper. Younger readers can catch up by pointing their mouse at YouTube. It's the sight and sound of distilled genius, however you look at it. As for the oft-mentioned mantra of 'I don't wanna live forever' (surely Lemmy's own version of The Who's 'Hope I die before I get old'), we want the exact opposite for him.

GENRES

Heavy metal

RECORDED

1980 in Rickmansworth, Hertfordshire

PRODUCER

Vic Maile

BAND MEMBERS

Ian 'Lemmy' Kilmister, 'Fast' Eddie Clarke, Phil 'Philthy Animal' Taylor

ON YOUTUBE  http://flametr.com/ace-of-motorhead

Scan to see a video on your smartphone (incl. iPhone & Android)

MUSE

PLUG IN BABY

Muse were an astonishing phenomenon when they first appeared on the international music scene. Their look, their instruments, the tones that they coaxed from those instruments, their clothes, their videos ... especially their videos, in particular the clip for 2002's single 'Plug In Baby', a horror movie for all the family. The opening riff of 'Plug In Baby', a twisty, finger-breaking little number which has gone on to top polls in several guitar magazines, is counterpointed by bassist Chris Wolstenholme's treated line and begins and ends in a flourish of electronic feedback. Rarely has a song about the emergence and domination of cyborg people, if indeed that is what singer Matt Bellamy is on about, sounded so dryly plausible, or been matched by such persuasive video images. The half-human, half writhing snake women who populate the video, which ends with Bellamy striking a tortured pose, are enough to make anyone sign up for Muse's frankly brilliant message. 'Plug In Baby' was only one of a string of fantastic, guitar-heavy singles from the band that continues to this day. There really is no one like them.

GENRES

Alternative rock, new prog, electronic rock

RECORDED

2001 in Dorking, Surrey

PRODUCER

David Bottrill, Muse

BAND MEMBERS

Matt Bellamy, Chris Wolstenholme, Dominic Howard

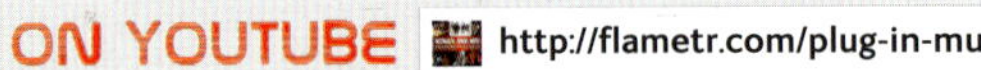

MUSE

HYSTERIA

By December 2003 Muse had established a huge audience for their unnervingly edgy brand of rock music, and the world was ready for one of their most complex works yet. 'Hysteria' begins with a bass riff that has become a modern classic, with Chris Wolstenholme issuing a microscopically precise line despite mountains of distortion. Guitarist Matt Bellamy picks up the riff and plays it in unison until the verses, where his guitar is muted. As anyone in a Muse covers band will know, playing this stuff isn't easy, composed as it is of multiple hammer-ons around the 12th fret. A low action is essential, no matter whether you're doing your best Muse impression on a guitar or a bass. 'Hysteria' has become a song which Muse crowds bay for whenever the band play live, thanks to that addictively snaky figure, its anthemic chorus and the funky backbeat which anchors the whole thing. As with 'Stairway To Heaven' or 'Ace Of Spades', the group will always have to include it in their set list, or risk angering their fans.

GENRES

Alternative rock, new prog, progressive metal

RECORDED

2002–03 in Westmeath, Ireland

PRODUCER

Rich Costey, Muse

BAND MEMBERS

Matt Bellamy, Chris Wolstenholme, Dominic Howard

NIRVANA

SMELLS LIKE TEEN SPIRIT

'It sounds too poppy,' mourned Nirvana front man Kurt Cobain in October 1991, when 'Smells Like Teen Spirit', the first single from his band's second album, *Nevermind*, was issued. He had a point. Compared to Nirvana's previous, relatively lo-fi recordings, 'Smells ...' was a glittering audio experience, all layered guitars and smooth drum rolls. On the other hand, this was apparently just what Generation X, the so-called 'slackers' ordered. 'Smells Like Teen Spirit' was Nirvana's biggest song and is in fact the biggest song ever to come out of the grunge scene. It stands tall today as the *de facto* anthem of grunge, which itself came crashing to a halt when Cobain committed suicide in April 1994.

RECORDING AND RELEASE

'Smells Like Teen Spirit' represents the most economical use of a single riff in more or less any song in this book. The riff, which opens the song as a solo guitar figure, is played in unison by the band in the choruses and is then replayed on bass only during the verses. It is a simple F, B♭, A♭, D♭ line in sixteenths and is perhaps the 1990s' most easily identifiable guitar riff. Cobain asked producer Butch Vig (later the drummer in Garbage) to multi-track his overdriven guitar tracks for a heavier sound, a feat which Vig pulled off with aplomb.

The single, released by Geffen subsidiary DGC Records, came with a video clip that managed to become a cultural meme in its own right, with its dark tones and angst-ridden close-ups often copied by bands well into the alt-rock and nu-metal era. Against a backdrop of cheerleaders and high-school bleachers, Cobain was pictured, screaming his lyrics in utter, miserable defiance. Both song and clip spoke directly to a bored, frustrated generation of young

rock fans, and it has never been off MTV. The death of Cobain aged only 27 has lent the song a certain heavyweight gravitas that the singer probably never envisioned.

MUSICAL LEGACY

Musical legacy? This song defines the term. 'Smells Like Teen Spirit' was by far the biggest rock song to come out of America – hell, out of the entire world – in 1991. Phrases such as 'anthem for a generation' are still common when people attempt to describe its impact. Praise be to whichever deity governs the electric guitar world, as cover versions of 'Smells ...' have been few and far between outside club bands. The day you hear Puff 'Every Breath You Take' Daddy sampling Cobain's riff for some nauseatingly tawdry R&B single will be the day that Aberdeen, Washington freezes over. Whether this is down to the decisions of the controllers of Nirvana's legacy (Grohl, Novoselic and Cobain's widow Courtney Love) is not known but, whatever the truth, the song's legacy has been so far safeguarded well. It has appeared on a couple of Nirvana box sets and live albums and that's basically it, with the video still much viewed on YouTube. Perhaps Cobain himself would have been proud of that.

GENRES

Grunge

RECORDED

1991 in Los Angeles

PRODUCER

Butch Vig

BAND MEMBERS

Kurt Cobain, Krist Novoselic, Dave Grohl

ON YOUTUBE 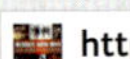 http://flametr.com/smells-teen-spirit

TED NUGENT

STRANGLEHOLD

In 1975 the American rock scene was invaded by a new force, a huntin', shootin', guitar-totin' hotshot called Ted Nugent, whose passion for blues rock was equalled only by his love of outdoor pursuits and his distaste for drunks and drug users (the last an unusual attitude for a 1970s rocker). Nugent's self-titled album contained many a career-best song, not least 'Cat Scratch Fever', his signature tune, as well as 'Stranglehold'. The latter functioned as a vehicle for his band to stretch out and jam, and as a background for the Motor City Madman's excellent lead guitar skills. The riff that introduces the song is utterly memorable. It's interesting to note that the song's extended mid-section, in which Nugent solos, would be perfect entertainment for blissed-out hippies, in diametric opposition to its composer's intentions. In later years 'Stranglehold' found a home on TV soundtracks and in the *Guitar Hero* video game franchise, although these days Nugent is better known for his political and social commentary than his guitar playing.

GENRES

Hard rock, psychedelic rock, blues rock

RECORDED

1975 in Atlanta

PRODUCER

Tom Werman, Lew Futterman

BAND MEMBERS

Derek St. Holmes, Ted Nugent, Rob Grange, Cliff Davies

ON YOUTUBE  http://flametr.com/stranglehold-nugent

ROY ORBISON

OH, PRETTY WOMAN

Inspired by a comment he'd heard regarding his wife that ran along the lines of 'A pretty woman never needs any money' (equal rights for women were clearly still some years away), operatic crooner Roy Orbison penned this all-time classic song and scored a hit in the UK among other territories. He'd already built a fan base – in the sense that such a thing could exist in the largely communications-free environment of the 1960s – with earlier hits such as 'Only The Lonely', and in 1964 the rock'n'roll world was ready for some more of his astounding voice.

While 'Oh, Pretty Woman' was a hit in its time and remained in the public eye (or ear, at least) for some years, the song's presence diminished as the decades passed. However, Hollywood had its eye on the song. Who could have predicted that a 1990s film would be the catalyst that gave 'Oh, Pretty Woman' (as literally no one called it any more) the boost that would make it a global hit, two decades and more after its initial release?

RECORDING AND RELEASE

Joined by a bevy of session guitarists, Roy Orbison recorded 'Oh, Pretty Woman' in 1964, having toured with the song for some time previously. (None other than The Beatles claimed to have seen Orbison play it live long before the single itself was released.) The classic, jangling opening riff, reminiscent of fellow rockabilly janglists Dick Dale and Duane Eddy, was an instant invitation to get one's hips on the dance floor, just at a time when beat music was being replaced by more demanding fashions such as the impending psychedelia. In fact, the success of 'Oh, Pretty Woman' a few years after its style was strictly in fashion is proof that a good song will triumph regardless of

changing times. Indeed, all these years later the song is still regarded – rightly – as an essential and priceless artefact from the mid-1960s.

MUSICAL LEGACY

'Oh, Pretty Woman' was largely forgotten before Julia Roberts and Richard Gere brought it back to life with the 1990s romantic comedy *Pretty Woman*. Curiously, the film was at heart a rather dark tale of exploitation and the abuse of power, but its big-name cast and feel-good factor (with the aid of Orbison's song) won huge audiences. Suddenly the title was back in common parlance, and Orbison – who had returned to the public eye thanks to his membership of the rock supergroup the Traveling Wilburys – would have benefited immensely, had he not succumbed to a heart attack in 1988. The song became his epitaph, sullied not at all by a lawsuit by Orbison's publisher, Acuff-Rose Music, against the rap group 2 Live Crew the following year. The rappers had recorded a parody of 'Oh, Pretty Woman' and won the case, leading to what is regarded by legal experts as an important precedent for the definition of 'fair use' in recorded music.

GENRES

Rockabilly

RECORDED

1964 in Nashville

PRODUCER

Fred Foster

BAND MEMBERS

Roy Orbison, Billy Sanford, Jerry Kennedy, Wayne Moss

ON YOUTUBE

Gibson

OZZY OSBOURNE

CRAZY TRAIN

Ozzy Osbourne was a household name in the 1970s, firstly as the singer with seminal heavy-metal originators Black Sabbath, but by 1979 he was out of the band, unemployed, miserable and wallowing in booze and cocaine. His saviour was Sharon Arden, the daughter of Sabbath's manager Don Arden, who offered to manage him. Together the future husband and wife assembled a solo band for Ozzy, including bassist and lyricist Bob Daisley, drummer Lee Kerslake and – the jewel in the crown – a young guitar prodigy called Randy Rhoads, who had played in a Californian club band called Quiet Riot. Rhoads brought a fistful of amazing riffs to the table, and the new band gathered to turn them into songs for a debut album called *Blizzard Of Ozz*. Ozzy had everything to prove and, in September 1980, he proved it.

RECORDING AND RELEASE

'Crazy Train', the first single from *Blizzard Of Ozz*, begins with a catchy, hammered-on riff that is as dexterous as it is memorable. Randy Rhoads brought the riff with him from his Quiet Riot days and applied it seamlessly to the rest of the song, which also features his incredibly fast solo with tapped, Eddie Van Halen-style sections. Lyrically, Ozzy is exhorting the listener to give up on hate and have a go at love instead, a sentiment at least a decade out of date by 1980, but which sounds perfectly appropriate in this upbeat rock song. Note that Rhoads double-tracked the vast majority of his guitar solos as well as his riffs, without missing a beat or making them sound like anything other than a single line. This was a measure of his playing excellence and focus, when time was pressing and budgets were low. After all, at this time Ozzy Osbourne was an unknown quantity as a solo artist, and the risk of him vanishing into oblivion if the project didn't pay off was very real.

RIDGE FARM

MUSICAL LEGACY

'Crazy Train' was the much-needed hit that ushered Ozzy into solo stardom. Rhoads, too, was instantly popular with fans, thanks to his youthful good looks, his incredible skills and the amazing story of how he had been plucked from obscurity. A series of singles and another Ozzy album, *Diary Of A Madman*, increased the stock of Ozzy/Randy/Sharon partnership still further, and the success of the new band would doubtless have continued had fate not intervened.

On 19 March 1982, Rhoads climbed aboard a single-engined aircraft in Florida for a quick aerial photo session. The pilot, Ozzy's tour bus driver, lost control of the plane and crashed it into a building, killing all aboard. Rhoads was only 25. His music lives on in Ozzy's solo career, with 'Crazy Train' in particular gaining new life when used on the soundtrack of MTV series *The Osbournes* in 2000. The version used was an easy-listening cover, recorded by 1960s crooner Pat Boone. You really couldn't make any of this story up.

GENRES

Heavy metal

RECORDED

1980 in Surrey

PRODUCER

Max Norman

BAND MEMBERS

Ozzy Osbourne, Randy Rhoads, Bob Daisley, Lee Kerslake

http://flametr.com/crazy-train

PANTERA

A NEW LEVEL

Heavy metal was changing its stripes when 1992 rolled around, and the groove was where it was at. Pantera, Machine Head and Sepultura were the first metal bands to introduce a touch of the ol' hipsway into their riffs, and arguably it was the first of these who did it best. After a major-label album called *Cowboys From Hell* in 1990, the Texas foursome had found their sound and attacked it with full commitment with *Vulgar Display Of Power* two years later. The record was one of those rarities that don't have a duff track, and 'A New Level' – the second song on the album – was truly mighty. Bolting together several killer riffs, the song featured an utterly mesmerizing chromatic figure that rose up the neck in increments (specifically, fretted 012, 0123, 01234, 6666) and added great tension to the song. Note how guitarist 'Dimebag' Darrell Abbott plays the riff in two ways, firstly with ringing power chords and then with crunching palm-muting. Believe it or not, Madonna covers that riff on stage from time to time – a slightly surreal experience.

GENRE

Groove metal, heavy metal

RECORDED

1991 in Pantego, Texas

PRODUCER

Terry Date

BAND MEMBERS

Phil Anselmo, 'Dimebag' Darrell Abbott, Rex Brown, Vinnie Paul Abbott

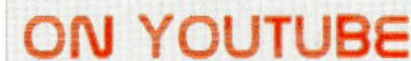

http://flametr.com/a-new-level

PANTERA

WALK

In 1993 nu-metal was on the way and grunge was on its way out. Somewhere in the middle of these angst-ridden movements lay the new groove-metal sound pioneered by Pantera, the hard-drinking quartet from Arlington, Texas, who had released four laughable glam albums in the 1980s before considerably toughening up their sound, signing to Atlantic subsidiary Atco and releasing their major-label debut LP, *Cowboys From Hell*.

By 1992 the follow-up album, *Vulgar Display Of Power*, was in stores and attracting the faithful in tens of thousands to this new, still heavy but slightly funky metal approach. The band, and primarily guitarist extraordinaire 'Dimebag' Darrell Abbott, were at the absolute peak of their powers – young and hungry for the kill, but sophisticated enough to know that metal with groove would pull in a bigger audience, for the simple reason that girls liked it too. Nowhere did this slinky, modern approach pay off better than in the song 'Walk'.

RECORDING AND RELEASE

'Walk on home, boy!' sneers singer Phil Anselmo as 'Walk' draws to a close, and well he might, having just delivered one of the era's most recognizable metal anthems. Based on a 'walking' guitar riff that strolls inexorably forward, the song is so simple that it hurts, with its commands of 'Respect!' and a stripped-down two-note progression. Dimebag's guitar sound, clipped to the maximum by expert palm-muting and quite possibly a noisegate applied by producer Terry Date, could have been made by a machine, so few are the imperfections in its performance. Check out his sustain, too; when Dimebag allows a chord to ring in the first bar of each chorus, it sounds as if it's going

to ring for days. The drums and bass are locked into the riff with incredible precision, too. Outstanding work for a band made up of resolute outsiders, you'll agree.

MUSICAL LEGACY

'Walk' has been covered by several metal bands, with most exposure by Avenged Sevenfold, the Californian quintet. It's easy to play and instantly recognizable, hence its popularity as a cover, but sadly it is unlikely that we'll hear any members of Pantera playing it. The band suffered a classic rise and fall career path, releasing three more albums after *Vulgar Display* ... before splitting amid personal friction. A war of words in the press was never resolved, as Dimebag was shot and killed on stage in December 2004 in Columbus, Ohio, by a disturbed ex-Marine. He had been playing in a new band called Damageplan with his brother Vinnie Paul, who now tours as a member of Hellyeah. Rex Brown and Phil Anselmo formed Down before the former quit to join a supergroup, Kill Devil Hill. Relations between the three survivors are yet to improve. Here's one re-formation that cannot happen for obvious reasons, although songs like 'Walk' will always be around to remind metal fans of the past glories of this most mercurial of bands.

GENRES

Groove metal, heavy metal

RECORDED

1991 in Pantego, Texas

PRODUCER

Terry Date

BAND MEMBERS

Phil Anselmo, 'Dimebag' Darrell Abbott, Rex Brown, Vinnie Paul Abbott

ON YOUTUBE http://flametr.com/walk-pantera

QUEEN

TIE YOUR MOTHER DOWN

Asked why Queen guitarist Brian May had written a song called 'Tie Your Mother Down', singer Freddie Mercury mused for a second and then suggested that perhaps May was feeling 'vicious' that day – an unlikely claim, given May's famously relaxed demeanour. Then again, the song does start with a high-register wail and a series of guitar layers that make it one of Queen's heavier songs, so there must have been something good in May's studio tea that day. After the opening figures, the song goes into a rock'n'roll boogie riff that sustains it for its duration. It remains a high point of the excellent 1976 album *A Day At The Races*, Queen's fifth album, alongside the much more passive 'Somebody To Love' and 'Good Old Fashioned Lover Boy', both of which are more or less the polar opposite of the rambunctious, headbanging 'Tie Your Mother Down'. If the mighty Queen can be summed up at all, it would be reasonable to tag them as a band who could do anything, as this song so amply demonstrates.

GENRE

Rock

RECORDED

1976 in London and Oxfordshire

PRODUCER

Queen

BAND MEMBERS

Freddie Mercury, Brian May, John Deacon, Roger Taylor

ON YOUTUBE  http://flametr.com/tie-your-queen

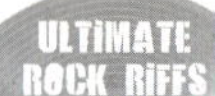

QUEENS OF THE STONE AGE

NO ONE KNOWS

In a flash, it seemed – although it was more likely the two-year period between 2000 and 2002 – Queens Of The Stone Age went from an unknown solo project to a global rock phenomenon. The group's second and third albums, *Rated R* and *Songs For The Deaf*, established them as contenders in this period, thanks to a clutch of killer singles, the best-known of which remains 'No One Knows'. Josh Homme's razor-sharp riff, punctuated with harmonics and slides, will forever be associated with the accompanying video in which the band – at this point a supergroup featuring Screaming Trees and Foo Fighters members – are kidnapped by a sinister animatronic deer on a hunting trip. The darkness behind the images suited the song perfectly. A few years before this, Homme had been holding down guitar duties in the superb desert-rock band Kyuss. When that band ground to a halt, few fans would have predicted that he would be playing stripped-down radio rock as perfectly as this. You can't keep a good man down, evidently.

GENRES

Hard rock, stoner rock

RECORDED

2002 in Los Angeles and San Rafael, California

PRODUCER

Josh Homme, Eric Valentine

BAND MEMBERS

Josh Homme, Mark Lanegan, Nick Oliveri, Dave Grohl

ON YOUTUBE  http://flametr.com/no-one-queens

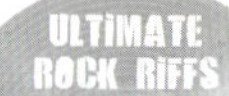

RAGE AGAINST THE MACHINE

WAKE UP

There is a lot to be said for playing a riff made of a single note, and in November 1992 Los Angeles rap-metallers Rage Against The Machine proved this dictum when they recorded 'Wake Up', which begins in exactly that way. With its determined, unison attack, that opening riff was likened by more than one listener to Led Zeppelin's 'Kashmir', although the two songs aren't otherwise similar. Rage Against The Machine singer Zack de la Rocha gave a career-best performance on this song, shrieking 'Wake up!' like some kind of dreadlocked demon as the song closes. Little wonder it was chosen to soundtrack the end of the 1999 sci-fi epic *The Matrix*, tying in neatly as it does with that film's themes of the unthinking slavery of the masses and their exploitation by corporations and governments (perennial tropes in Rage Against The Machine's music). Elsewhere the song references FBI director J. Edgar Hoover and Martin Luther King, Jr, among other historical figures. This was serious stuff, reflected in the direction and repetition of that sinister, single-minded riff, and in line with the message of the seminal, self-titled album on which it appeared.

GENRES

Rap metal, funk metal, alternative metal

RECORDED

1992 in Los Angeles

PRODUCER

Garth Richardson

BAND MEMBERS

Zack de la Rocha, Tom Morello, Tim Commerford, Brad Wilk

ON YOUTUBE  http://flametr.com/wake-up-rage

RAGE AGAINST THE MACHINE

KILLING IN THE NAME

The most famous song ever to emerge from the rap-metal scene, Limp Bizkit notwithstanding, doesn't actually have that much rapping in it. 'Killing In The Name', released ahead of Rage Against The Machine's self-titled debut album, is based on a single, anti-Ku Klux Klan diatribe expressed in a simple couple of sentences barked out by singer Zack de la Rocha. The main riff, an instantly addictive number expressed in drop-D tuning by guitarist Tom Morello, runs through the song, giving way to the choruses and the fantastic outro section in which de la Rocha repeats 'F*** you, I won't do what you tell me' all the way to the end. This final section caused the song to be banned on Radio One in the UK when DJ Bruno Brooks played it, unaware of its content. Live, the song is one of the most adrenalized experiences any audience member can ever enjoy. Fortunately for us, Rage Against The Machine are still in business and don't seem to be going anywhere soon.

GENRES

Rap metal, funk metal, alternative metal

RECORDED

1992 in Los Angeles

PRODUCER

Garth Richardson

BAND MEMBERS

Zack de la Rocha, Tom Morello, Tim Commerford, Brad Wilk

ON YOUTUBE  http://flametr.com/killing-rage

RAZORLIGHT

IN THE MORNING

Truly the Noughties were the decade in which post-punk came back, and nowhere were the legacies of Television, Wire and Talking Heads more honoured than with Razorlight's second album, released in 2006. The opening track, 'In The Morning', is founded on a clean, sixteenths-based riff that harks directly back to the class of New York of 1983, and is eminently hummable, enabling the song to become a major hit. Although Razorlight never really abandoned their indie roots, it was felt in some quarters that the self-titled album's more commercial sound was in some ways a betrayal of their fans. Punters begged to disagree, buying *Razorlight* in huge quantities and establishing the band as one of a wave of indie acts for the new millennium. Since then 'In The Morning' has become a fan favourite when played live, in much the same way that 'Take Me Out' (also in this book) did for Franz Ferdinand. Indeed, the two songs' key riffs have a lot in common, specifically the down strokes punctuating the kick drum.

GENRES

Indie rock

RECORDED

2006 in London

PRODUCER

Chris Thomas

BAND MEMBERS

Johnny Borrell, Gus Robertson, Freddie Stitz, David Sullivan Kaplan

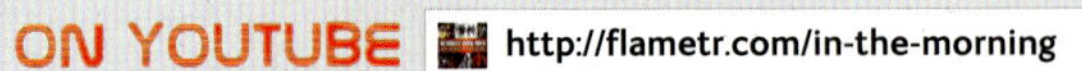

RED HOT CHILI PEPPERS

UNDER THE BRIDGE

In spring 1992, the Hollywood funk-rock quartet the Red Hot Chili Peppers took a turn away from their usual rappin', frontin', jumpin'-about-on-stage routine and released a ballad, 'Under The Bridge'. Devoid of slap bass or lyrics about sex for a change, 'Under The Bridge' was a tender song devoted to the Los Angeles location where singer Anthony Kiedis first savoured the dubious pleasures of heroin. Guitar-wise, the song was a marvel, based on John Frusciante's untreated clean tone and unravelling beautifully from the chordal riff that opened it. Later in the song, Frusciante layers simple, complementary lines over the main chords, keeping his parts effective and allowing the more melodic components of the song – such as a female choir – to shine through.

RECORDING AND RELEASE

After 1989's excellent *Mother's Milk* album, the Chilis felt that a change of direction and recording venue was in order, and recruited superbeard Rick Rubin (who had previously produced albums by the Beastie Boys, Slayer and other seminal bands) to helm the console at his studio in Hollywood. Moving into the house and trailing recording equipment up and down stairwells, band and producer created the perfect recording environment for their new album. 'Under The Bridge' was initially not considered for the album, eventually titled *Blood Sugar Sex Magik*, because composer Kiedis felt that it was too sensitive to stand alongside the other, more aggressive songs. Rubin persuaded him to record it. A wise decision, as it was an enormous hit on its release. 'Under The Bridge' is now the Chilis' signature song, alongside other high-impact tunes from *Blood Sugar Sex Magik* such as 'Give It Away'.

MUSICAL LEGACY

'Under The Bridge' marked a sea change for the Red Hot Chili Peppers in several ways. First, it enabled them to be taken seriously as a band who wrote subtle, emotional songs, the opposite of their image up until that point. It also demonstrated that there was still an appetite among the public for songs that actually said something rather than merely being about surface pyrotechnics. Most importantly, 'Under The Bridge' marked the beginning of a new, commercial era for the Chilis. A 1993 single called 'Soul To Squeeze' used very similar chords and songs of the same, soft-edged nature appear regularly on Chili Peppers albums released since then. After a sticky 1990s, during which the group went through different guitarists, Frusciante returned to the band and recorded a comeback album, 1999's *Californication*, loaded with the same mellow guitar tones as 'Under The Bridge'. Proof indeed that a winning formula shouldn't be abandoned. The song returned to the public eye in 1998 when UK girl band All Saints covered it, although they managed to ruin the opening riff by sampling and looping it unnecessarily and delivering the lyrics in a winsome R&B style. At least 'Under The Bridge' lives on through the Chilis' live performances, which continued at stadium level through the 2000s, until the departure once more of Frusciante and the hiatus which is still in place at the time of writing.

GENRES

Alternative rock

RECORDED

1991 in Los Angeles

PRODUCER

Rick Rubin

BAND MEMBERS

Anthony Kiedis, John Frusciante, Michael 'Flea' Balzary, Chad Smith

ON YOUTUBE  http://flametr.com/under-bridge

THE ROLLING STONES

(I CAN'T GET NO) SATISFACTION

Perhaps The Rolling Stones' best-known song, '(I Can't Get No) Satisfaction' was released in May 1965 and caused something of a storm of controversy among the moral guardians of the day. As well as referring in fairly specific terms to a lack of success with the ladies, singer Mick Jagger attacked the advertisement culture of the mid-1960s with some acutely aimed barbs that caused more than a few authorities to purse their lips in disapproval. We look back and laugh now at such outdated ethical pettiness, but back then The Rolling Stones were treading a fine line that could (and often did) get them into serious trouble. We're fortunate that they did.

RECORDING AND RELEASE

The famous opening riff of '(I Can't Get No) Satisfaction' was recorded by Keith Richards with the aid of a Gibson fuzzbox to give it extra crunch and sustain, not because The Stones or producer Andrew Loog Oldham were looking for a more rocked-up sound but because the idea was to simulate a horn line. Intending to replace the initial guitar part with horns in the final recording, Richards was surprised when Oldham and the rest of the band voted to keep the original guitar riff. As he later explained, he had come up with the original three-note riff on an acoustic while jamming one night, and recorded himself doing so without any explicit intention of turning it into a song. The riff was given great power by bassist Bill Wyman, who joins in after only a single bar. For added presence, check out the stereo version of the song on YouTube, which features an acoustic guitar and piano higher in the mix than the original mono recording.

MUSICAL LEGACY

'(I Can't Get No) Satisfaction' annoyed an older and/or more conservative audience for several reasons, although nowadays the song seems pretty tame. First, Jagger sang about failing to secure any 'girl reaction', a reference to his success with women that some found just too graphic to tolerate. Worse, he referred to a particular girl being unwilling to partake in amorous activity with him because she's 'on a losing streak', which some listeners interpreted as indicating the status of her menstrual cycle. Finally, and most damningly given that the song was a big hit in 1960s America, where the ethos of the day was basically 'Spend, spend, spend!', Jagger criticized the man on the radio who tries to sell him a brand of cigarettes and values a particularly white shirt. This was a big deal in that the lyrics implied that the shiny, successful, post-war world based on teenage dollars and consumer spending was valueless to a band like The Stones. Little wonder that '(I Can't Get No) Satisfaction' ruffled some feathers. The line 'trying to make some girl' was deemed too rude for radio and TV broadcast and was censored as a result, an amusing concept today, when The Stones regularly perform '(I Can't Get No) Satisfaction' in all its supposedly profane glory at events such as the Superbowl.

GENRES

Rock'n'roll, hard rock, garage rock

RECORDED

1965 in Los Angeles

PRODUCER

Andrew Loog Oldham

BAND MEMBERS

Mick Jagger, Keith Richards, Brian Jones, Bill Wyman, Charlie Watts

ON YOUTUBE  http://flametr.com/satisfaction-stones

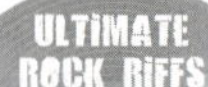

THE ROLLING STONES

JUMPIN' JACK FLASH

In 1968 The Rolling Stones were in a period of transition, having weathered the previous year's Summer Of Love with their collective sanity mostly intact. They were looking for the next flash of inspiration now that the wave of British psychedelia had begun to fade. In retrospect, we know now that the Altamont tragedy and a decade full of stadium-level success awaited them, most of it in America, but at the time the group simply did what they did best and issued a rootsy single, 'Jumpin' Jack Flash'. Inspired by guitarist Keith Richards' country-house gardener, Jack, who had inadvertently awoken singer Mick Jagger one morning, the song begins with a classic, rolling blues riff, which bassist Bill Wyman claimed to have written on a piano and contributed without credit. As for the lyrics, Jagger later stated that they were merely written in reaction to the acid frenzy that had surrounded The Stones' 1967 psych album *Their Satanic Majesties Request* ...

RECORDING AND RELEASE

Keith Richards played the riff on two acoustic guitars, one tuned to open D with a capo, although he later replaced this for live performances with a guitar tuned to open G using a capo on the fourth fret. And what live performances there have been. The song didn't appear on a regular, non-compilation Stones LP, but it has been a high point of every live album recorded by the band and is still one of their essential set-list inclusions to this day. A couple of promo videos were filmed for the song in 1968, an unusually early marketing move even for a band as cash-rich as The Rolling Stones. They depict a young, naïve group who obviously know roughly what they're doing with their talents but not, perhaps, what their future holds.

MUSICAL LEGACY

A UK No. 1, 'Jumpin' Jack Flash' has subsequently appeared on several film soundtracks and been adopted as the walk-on music for baseball players, but it has rarely suffered the indignity of a terrible cover version. It's such an original, roots-based song that more or less anyone with a command of the blues can cover it reasonably well, with early adopters of the song including Leon Russell (who performed it at George Harrison's Concert For Bangladesh in 1971), Johnny Winter, the Beach Boys, Peter Frampton and Tina Turner. Aretha Franklin also gave the song a soul makeover. More modern takes on the classic Stones ditty include one by Motörhead, whose singer Lemmy is a rock'n'roll enthusiast to the core (and is only two years younger than Richards, making the two virtual contemporaries), and another by Guns N' Roses, who made a demo cut of 'Jumpin' Jack Flash' in 1987. Then there are Britpop versions, covers by reality-TV stars, even a sitar-based version by Ananda Shankar. 'Jumpin' Jack Flash' really is a song that transcends generations and musical styles. Expect it to remain part of the fabric of popular rock culture for decades to come.

GENRES

Hard rock

RECORDED

1968 in London

PRODUCER

Jimmy Miller

BAND MEMBERS

Mick Jagger, Keith Richards, Brian Jones, Bill Wyman, Charlie Watts, Nicky Hopkins, Jimmy Miller

ON YOUTUBE  http://flametr.com/jumpin-jack

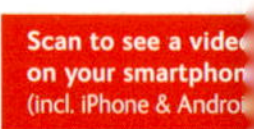

HIWATT

THE ROLLING STONES

BROWN SUGAR

'God knows what I'm on about on that song,' said Rolling Stones singer Mick Jagger, asked about his band's remarkable 1971 single, 'Brown Sugar'. 'It's such a mishmash. All the nasty subjects in one go.... I would never write that song now. I would probably censor myself. I'd think, "Oh God, I can't. I've got to stop".' So what were these 'nasty subjects', you ask? Well, here Jagger appears to be addressing the immortal subjects of interracial sex, S&M and heroin – pretty standard fare as rock inspirations these days, but less so back in the Seventies, when pop music was regarded as for light entertainment purposes only. Ignoring all that, however, 'Brown Sugar' is a marvellous truckload of riffs bolted together by Stax-style horn lines, yelped falsetto backing vocals and an immensely funky groove that swings, as Jagger might have put it himself, like a madman. Whether the inspiration for the title, Jagger's African-American lover Marsha Hunt, felt complimented by the song, is a matter for conjecture.

RECORDING AND RELEASE

'Brown Sugar' was devoured by rock buyers on its release in April 1971, hitting the top of the US singles chart and peaking at No. 2 in the UK. The parent album, *Sticky Fingers*, was one of a seminal sequence of Rolling Stones LPs released in the late Sixties and early Seventies, and 'Brown Sugar' was symptomatic of the rich seam of inspiration that the band were exploring at the time. The naughty themes of the song were masked from the most innocent ears by metaphors, but nonetheless Jagger felt the need to amend the more obvious lines in subsequent live performances. Note that the lines 'Just like a young girl should' and 'Hear him whip the women just around midnight' tend to morph into 'Just like a young man should' and 'You shoulda heard him just around midnight'.

MUSICAL LEGACY

'Brown Sugar' is one of the last songs recorded by The Rolling Stones as a raw, blues-rock act. You can hear their club background in the execution of the music, which focuses on emotion and audience connection rather than precision-engineered performances. Its groove is its main strength, which explains the power of 'Brown Sugar' to energize concertgoers and to fill dancefloors. After this point, The Stones gradually began a move towards slick, stadium-rock territory, which they have occupied ever since the mid-Seventies. Guitarist Mick Taylor, a blues expert, laid down a fantastic guitar part on 'Brown Sugar', full of the warmth and panache for which he is famous, but he quit in 1974 after disagreements with Keith Richards. His place was taken by ex-Faces guitarist Ronnie Wood, who remains with The Stones to this day. While Wood is an astounding multi-instrumentalist, Jagger and others have paid tribute to Taylor as the most musical person ever to have been a Rolling Stone. The times they were a-changing, and 'Brown Sugar' came at the tail end of one era and the beginning of another.

GENRES

Hard rock

RECORDED

1969 in Muscle Shoals, Alabama

PRODUCER

Jimmy Miller

BAND MEMBERS

Mick Jagger, Keith Richards, Mick Taylor, Bill Wyman, Charlie Watts

ON YOUTUBE  http://flametr.com/brown-sugar-stones

THE ROLLING STONES

START ME UP

By 1981 The Rolling Stones had evolved into the stadium-packing outfit that we know today, and the music they were making was a long way from the unformed blues that had thrilled audiences as late as the mid-Seventies. They still had what it took to write a decent rock anthem, though, and as the Eighties dawned one came along in the form of 'Start Me Up', with its irresistible opening riff. Brash and unapologetic, the song made it clear that the 1980s would be the decade in which The Stones found their maximum audience, as indeed history proved. In 1994 Microsoft paid the band a number rumoured to be in eight figures (in dollars, mind) to use the song in its marketing campaign for the then-revolutionary Windows 95 operating system, although the exact amount Bill Gates paid to Jagger, Richards et al. has not been revealed. Based on the success of Windows 95, though, which made Microsoft a bigger earner than The Beatles, The Stones and Elvis Presley combined, the sum was a shrewd investment.

GENRES

Hard rock

RECORDED

1981 in New York

PRODUCER

Mick Jagger, Keith Richards

BAND MEMBERS

Mick Jagger, Keith Richards, Ron Wood, Bill Wyman, Charlie Watts

ON YOUTUBE 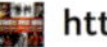 http://flametr.com/start-me-stones

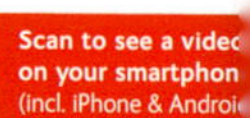

RUSH

THE SPIRIT OF RADIO

Every now and then a traditionally 'difficult' band produces a song that is different from its normal output. Simple and easily digestible, the song becomes a hit and said band is then forced to play it for the rest of their careers, even though it doesn't represent their normal sound. 'The Spirit Of Radio' is Rush's version of this song. Anthemic, relatively uncomplicated in riffs and arrangement and hardly obsessed with fantasy and science fiction, 'Spirit ...' was a vast hit on its appearance in 1980, ushering in a regrettable era for the Canadian prog-rock trio that was typified by rolled-up jacket sleeves, mullets and synthesizers. Still, it was the Eighties (what did *you* look like back then?) and anyway, 'The Spirit Of Radio' is an absolutely magnificent song. Beginning with guitarist Alex Lifeson's scintillating barrage of notes, the song cuts in and out of a four-chord verse sequence, a reggaefied back end and the occasional musical flourish – as opposed to a standard Rush song from the Seventies, which was pretty much all about musical flourishes.

GENRES

Hard rock, progressive rock

RECORDED

1979 in Morin Heights, Quebec

PRODUCER

Rush, Terry Brown

BAND MEMBERS

Geddy Lee, Alex Lifeson, Neil Peart

ON YOUTUBE

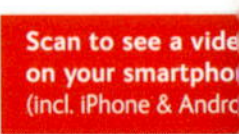

FRIENDLY

ED SHEERAN

LEGO HOUSE

The smooth cascade of notes that begins singer-songwriter Ed Sheeran's 2011 hit 'Lego House' introduces a song of great sensitivity, but with enough drive to get Sheeran's legions of fans on their feet. It's a slow-building story of obsession, as epitomized in the video by the performance of Rupert 'Ron Weasley' Grint, who plays a man for whom nothing else matters apart from the love of his life. With its slow build and subtle musicianship, 'Lego House' demonstrates Sheeran's knack for a gripping tune, and indeed it is this ability to incorporate winning melodies and plangent guitar tones that has elevated him to the position of Youthful Pop Star Most Likely To ... over the last couple of years. The album from which 'Lego House' came, the huge-selling + (pronounced 'Plus') contained further proof that the man knows what he's doing when it comes to the ol' six-string. Sheeran has courage, too. Would *you* be able to get up at the 2012 London Olympics opening ceremony and sing a Pink Floyd song alongside original members of the Floyd?

GENRES

Indie folk, pop rock, soul

RECORDED

2011 in Windlesham, Surrey

PRODUCER

Jake Gosling

BAND MEMBERS

Ed Sheeran, Chris Leonard, Ben Hollingsworth

ON YOUTUBE  http://flametr.com/lego-sheeran

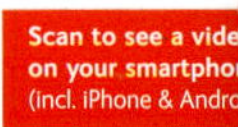

SLAYER

RAINING BLOOD

Compressing several impossible-to-play riffs into its four minutes (three if you discount the thunderstorm effects at the song's beginning and end), 'Raining Blood' is the final song on Slayer's finest album, *Reign In Blood* (see what they did there?). Like the opening track, 'Angel Of Death', 'Raining Blood' is almost too intense to describe in words, let alone to listen to at anything approaching high volume. The song's best-known riff is the descending line that begins the song, punctuated each bar by three power-chord hits, but the mesmerizingly brutal riff that precedes the vocals is also an all-time classic. The song, according to its writers Jeff Hanneman and Kerry King, is about Satan, who is seated in one of Hell's chambers. As he looks up towards the ceiling, which is composed of stalactites (bear with us here), blood from the lost souls impaled there drips downwards, hence the song title. Über-producer Rick Rubin, who produced *Reign In Blood*, added some rain effects, and the song has gone down in history as one of the most metal compositions ever recorded.

GENRES

Thrash metal

RECORDED

1986 in Los Angeles

PRODUCER

Rick Rubin

BAND MEMBERS

Tom Araya, Kerry King, Jeff Hanneman, Dave Lombardo

ON YOUTUBE  http://flametr.com/raining-blood

THE SONICS

HAVE LOVE, WILL TRAVEL

Garage rock was what your band played in 1965 if you didn't have a record deal or decent equipment but you still wanted to rock out. The Sonics, post-war kids born into austerity in Washington State, were more successful with the garage approach than most bands of their type, and made a splendid racket – most notably on this Richard Berry-penned tune from 1959. What makes the song and the blitzkrieg riff that opens it so special is the level of raucous overdrive applied to the guitar tone, when the sound was not yet common, and the small matter of said riff being impossible to forget once heard. When the punk movement had got underway a decade later, the song was pounced on by a number of well-known musicians, Stiv Bators among them. Bruce Springsteen also covered 'Have Love, Will Travel', and in recent years the blues-rock band the Black Keys drew renewed attention to it with their version. Fifty years old and counting, 'Have Love, Will Travel' is evidence that kids, no matter what their generation, have always wanted to rock out.

GENRES

Garage rock, proto-punk

RECORDED

1965 in Seattle

PRODUCER

Buck Ornsby, Kent Morrill

BAND MEMBERS

Gerry Roslie, Andy Parypa, Larry Parypa, Rob Lind, Bob Bennett

ON YOUTUBE  http://flametr.com/have-love

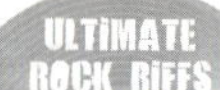

SOUNDGARDEN

OUTSHINED

It's odd to think that the mission of grunge was, initially at least, to rid the world of traditional heavy metal, because so much grunge was infused with the spirit of classic metal. Take Soundgarden's 1992 single 'Outshined'. It begins with a riff that is pure Black Sabbath circa 1972, albeit downtuned and played with a thoroughly modern picking precision. There is no getting away from it – this is a heavy metal song. Then again, Soundgarden were always the most metallic members of the classic grunge wave. Heavier than Nirvana, more introspective than Pearl Jam, less angst-ridden than Alice In Chains, the band absorbed their metal influences directly into their sound. Fans loved this approach and repaid the group's efforts by making 'Outshined' and the *Badmotorfinger* album from which it came into enduring hits. Soundgarden, who re-formed in 2011 after a 14-year hiatus, continue to plough the same heavyweight furrow with even more success than they enjoyed in the grunge era, quite possibly because singer Chris Cornell's solo work in the interim had been patchy at best.

GENRES

Grunge, heavy metal

RECORDED

1991 in Los Angeles and Sausalito, California and Woodinville, Washington

PRODUCER

Terry Date, Soundgarden

BAND MEMBERS

Chris Cornell, Kim Thayil, Ben Shepherd, Matt Cameron

http://flametr.com/outshined-sound

STEPPENWOLF

BORN TO BE WILD

'Heavy metal thunder!' wailed Steppenwolf singer John Kay in 1968, ushering in a new era of awareness for heavy music. The term heavy metal had been coined by rock journalist Lester Bangs before this, but Steppenwolf's biker anthem was the first song to place it in front of a widespread audience, making it a buzz phrase for a generation of hippies and garage bands. Bikers loved 'Born To Be Wild' and the pounding riff that anchored the song, a guitar and organ sound that later bands such as Deep Purple adopted. The song's appearance in the classic 1969 road movie *Easy Rider* cemented its position in the counterculture of the day and all these years later, the melody is still connected in many fans' minds with images of a burning chopper motorcycle and the Stars and Stripes. Cover versions by The Cult (good) and Slayer (terrible) have kept 'Born To Be Wild' in the public eye, despite the rise of mocking phrases such as 'Born To Be Mild', used to describe someone who tries, and fails, to rock.

GENRES

Blues rock, heavy metal, hard rock

RECORDED

1967 in Los Angeles

PRODUCER

Gabriel Mekler

BAND MEMBERS

John Kay, Rushton Moreve, Michael Monarch, Goldy McJohn, Jerry Edmonton

http://flametr.com/born-to-be-wolf

Rickenbacker

THE STOOGES

I WANNA BE YOUR DOG

Perhaps punk didn't start in 1976 after all. There's certainly a case for American rock bands such as The Stooges being the inventors of the form several years before punk's supposed Year Zero, especially when you take into account 'I Wanna Be Your Dog'. Based on a grinding G, F♯, E figure laden with walls of primitive distortion, the song is at once grimly nihilistic and hilarious, combining as it does Iggy Pop's laconic vocal and the histrionics of the rest of the band. Producer John Cale played a piano line to add to the overall droned effect, and the song was rapidly established as an anthem for a disaffected generation of kids for whom the hippie dream was fading fast. Along with The Ramones, The Stooges were the catalyst for the transformation of garage rock into punk, although this only became clear with hindsight. At the time, all the band and their followers knew was that it felt good to play hard, loud, messy music that didn't care about conventions or traditions. What better reason to form a band?

GENRES

Protopunk, garage rock, heavy metal

RECORDED

1969

PRODUCER

John Cale

BAND MEMBERS

Iggy Pop, Dave Alexander, Ron Asheton, Scott Asheton

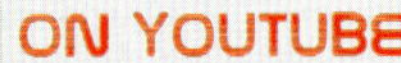

THE SURFARIS

WIPE OUT

Teen culture in 1963 was all about dance crazes, just as it is today. When surf music broke in America, it was huge, with the obvious proponents being the Beach Boys, but a relatively little-known group who played a huge part in the phenomenon were The Surfaris, four Californian kids whose novelty hit 'Wipe Out' has never really gone away in the half-century since its release. The irritating or amusing (choose one) laugh and falsetto wail of 'Wipe out!' that introduces the song was the signal back in the Sixties for massed dancefloor action, a call to arms repeated in 1987 when comedy rap trio the Fat Boys teamed up with some of the Beach Boys for a massively successful hit. It's interesting to note that 'Wipe Out' was originally issued as the throwaway B-side of a single called 'Surfer Joe'. The band and manager Dale Smallin (the guy who did the laugh) obviously failed to realize that comedy gold often leads to actual gold. Amazingly, a version of The Surfaris continues to play live shows today.

GENRES

Surf rock

RECORDED

1962 in Cucamonga, California

PRODUCER

Richard Delvy

BAND MEMBERS

Ron Wilson, Jim Fuller, Bob Berryhill, Pat Connolly

ON YOUTUBE http://flametr.com/wipe-out

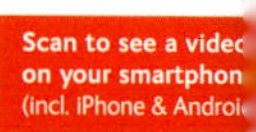

SONOR
SurFARIS

SURVIVOR

EYE OF THE TIGER

May 1982 saw the release of possibly the most macho song ever recorded, Survivor's 'Eye Of The Tiger'. Laden with testosterone and just a little bit camp, the song has managed not to sink into obscurity because it's so incredibly memorable. You'll never forget that quick-fire opening riff. A guitar pedals gently, drums build, and suddenly – zap! It's E! E-D-E! E-D-E! E-D-C! Like Rocky Balboa punching James 'Clubber' Lang right in the face 10 times as revenge for killing his faithful retainer and also for possessing that hairstyle, 'Eye Of The Tiger' is simple, to the point and perhaps a touch painful after several repetitions. People love the song, though, and not just because it evokes nostalgia for a day when day-glo socks were *de rigueur* and red-top newspapers told us that society would descend into chaos if we watched 'video nasties'. It's because, as themes for boxing films go, the song is unsurpassable, and there are no finer boxing movies than the first four *Rockys*, Robert De Niro's *Raging Bull* excepted.

RECORDING AND RELEASE

Sylvester Stallone himself requested that Survivor write 'Eye Of The Tiger', supposedly because he was unable to license Queen's 'Another One Bites The Dust' for use in the third Rocky film. In fact, 'Eye ...' is a better fit for the themes of the movie, which basically revolve around the metaphor of the 'eye of the tiger' as a dedicated frame of mind, rather useful when battling someone as hard as Mr T. The band considered various lyrics for the chorus before opting to throw in the title as its final line, simply because the hook was strong enough to attract the song's intended audience and didn't require any finessing. On its release, 'Eye Of The Tiger' sold in vast quantities, eventually shifting two million copies in the USA and becoming a *bona fide* sports anthem.

MUSICAL LEGACY

The reputation of 'Eye Of The Tiger' is closely linked to that of *Rocky III* itself. A decent standalone movie or when treated as the third installment of the franchise, it introduced the idea of boxer Rocky Balboa facing down a tougher, meaner opponent through the strength of his will. The series went downhill slightly after this, although Stallone fans will recall that the actor/director recruited Survivor once more for *Rocky IV*, which came out in 1985. The band's theme song, 'Burning Heart', failed to match up to the less-is-more ethos of 'Eye Of The Tiger', however. Cover versions barely exist, although we'd like to see someone do an easy listening or lounge 'Eye ...' sometime. That said, point your mouse at YouTube and search for 'pop idol eye of the tiger', where you will witness a hapless hopeful singing the song on a British TV talent show in front of judges such as Simon Cowell. The auditionee in question barks out the most hilarious version of the song ever, in front of his disbelieving jurors, before vanishing into a black hole made out of pure embarrassment. There's a lesson for us all there.

GENRES

Rock, hard rock

RECORDED

1982 in Los Angeles

PRODUCER

Frankie Sullivan

BAND MEMBERS

Dave Bickler, Frankie Sullivan, Jim Peterik, Stephan Ellis, Marc Droubay

ON YOUTUBE

SURVIVOR

THEM CROOKED VULTURES

MIND ERASER, NO CHASER

Get members of Led Zeppelin, Queens Of The Stone Age and the Foo Fighters in a band together and you'd expect some pretty meaty riffs to emerge, and emerge one did in November 2009 when Them Crooked Vultures released 'Mind Eraser, No Chaser'. John Homme worked his usual magic on guitar, building a funky line in unison with Zep bassist John Paul Jones, who (it must be said) strolled through the whole affair as if it was just another session. Some time later Dave Grohl, who recruited Jones to the band, was told by none other than Sir Paul McCartney that he, the sometime Beatle, would have been keen to join the band had Jones not got there first. The drummer had to tell Macca that his services were not required, but it's interesting to consider that the resulting Them Crooked Vultures songs might have been more melodic and less riff-driven had McCartney made the cut. As it is, Them Crooked Vultures are perhaps the most adept group of riff-writers ever assembled, although Jones, Grohl and Homme's previous bands Zeppelin, Nirvana and Kyuss all come pretty close.

GENRES

Alternative rock, hard rock

RECORDED

2009 in Los Angeles

PRODUCER

Them Crooked Vultures

BAND MEMBERS

Josh Homme, John Paul Jones, Dave Grohl

ON YOUTUBE  http://flametr.com/mind-eraser

THIN LIZZY

THE BOYS ARE BACK IN TOWN

'Bippin' and a boppin', tellin' a dirty joke or two' warbled Thin Lizzy singer Phil Lynott in April 1976, although he failed to clarify exactly how one 'bipped'. Nonetheless, the eponymous chaps in 'The Boys Are Back In Town' – to this day Lizzy's best-known single – seem to be having such a splendid time, doing whatever they're doing, that you can't help but buy into the song's message. Play hard, party, meet girls, have fun, and over the years the song has been attached to so many instances of macho swaggering and debauchery that it's impossible to list them all. The Irish national rugby team play the song when they run onto the pitch, appropriately so as Lynott was a son of Eire. The song also appeared on the soundtrack of the animated movie *Toy Story 2*, with the word 'boys' altered to resemble 'toys'. As well as the instantly recognizable opening riff, take note of the splendid dual guitar harmonies courtesy of Scott Gorham and Brian Robertson – one of Lizzy's most enduring contributions to the rock world.

GENRES

Hard rock

RECORDED

1975–76 in London

PRODUCER

John Alcock

BAND MEMBERS

Phil Lynott, Scott Gorham, Brian Robertson, Brian Downey

ON YOUTUBE  http://flametr.com/boys-back-town

Marshall

GEORGE THOROGOOD & THE DESTROYERS

BAD TO THE BONE

Released in September 1982, George Thorogood & The Destroyers' 'Bad To The Bone' was an anomaly in the age of chiffon scarves and Duran Duran. A savage piece of pure guitar blues, the song swaggered out of the blocks with a filthy but addictive guitar riff courtesy of Thorogood himself, and didn't leave until it had had its way with the listener. You will have heard the song used in many films, usually in scenes where a particularly unfriendly hard case walks menacingly into a bar. One famous scene in *Terminator 2* is a perfect example; when a 250-pound cyborg walks into a bar dressed in leather and begins killing people, you don't want to hear a song by Spandau Ballet.

RECORDING AND RELEASE

Despite its similarity to ancient blues standards by Chuck Berry, Elvis Presley and other legends, the opening riff of 'Bad To The Bone' was strong enough to make the song a reasonable-sized hit on its release. Its real success, however, came when MTV received its accompanying video and placed it on heavy rotation. In the clip, Thorogood is seen playing pool with bluesman Bo Diddley, whose previous work had included riffs that sounded a lot like 'Back To The Bone', now we come to think of it. As the game progresses, Thorogood works his way through an economy-sized cigar. When he places a shot at the eight ball at the climax, he drops a chunk of ash on the floor, which apparently causes the ball to fall into the pocket. As the man said, bad to the bone.

MUSICAL LEGACY

Despite its amusing video, 'Bad To The Bone' is a genuinely serious composition. However, a tendency remains for it to be used in a comedic or ironic way in the many films and TV shows in which it has been included. Its writers are no doubt rather relaxed about this as the royalties keep pouring in whichever way it's used. The song was used in the horror movie *Christine*, an adaptation of the Stephen King chiller of the same name, to denote the all-American car that was the leading character of the film. 'Bad To The Bone' was also featured heavily in an episode of the cult TV series *Miami Vice*, which in retrospect is simply one 1980s phenomenon paying tribute to another. Wrestlers, baseball players and martial arts fighters have also employed the song as walk-on themes, again with tongue deeply in cheek, and it has appeared in several TV commercials too. The most notable legacy of 'Bad To The Bone', apart from these regular reappearances in popular media, is its reaffirmation of the electric blues genre, however. Apart from the late Stevie Ray Vaughan and the still-extant Ted Nugent, George Thorogood & The Destroyers are probably the most successful purveyors of souped-up blues playing today, and without a shadow of a doubt it was 'Bad To The Bone' that put the band in that position.

GENRES

Blues rock

RECORDED

1981

PRODUCER

The Delaware Destroyers

BAND MEMBERS

George Thorogood, Billy Blough, Jeff Simon, Hank Carter, Ian Stewart

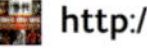
http://flametr.com/bad-bone

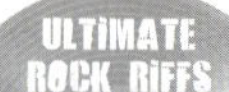

THE TROGGS

WILD THING

'Wild Thing' was released by English R&B foursome The Troggs in April 1966 and became one of their biggest hits, all without actually being written by the band. Originally composed by American singer-songwriter Chip Taylor and recorded by the Wild Ones the previous year, 'Wild Thing' was largely unknown until the Brits got hold of it and sold it back to the USA, where it became a No. 1 hit. Strange how pop music goes sometimes, but as long as all the money went to its rightful owners, what's the problem? Unfortunately the music business in the Sixties was not above a little corruption, in much the same way that the sea is not above the land.

RECORDING AND RELEASE

'Wild Thing' is based on a classic I-IV-V-IV riff that is so simple, it is difficult to conceive of a time in musical history when it hadn't been used and reused dozens of times, as is the case today. However, the riff sounded completely new and fresh in 1965, especially when you added the super-cool call-and-response sections that began 'Wild thing ... I think I love you'. Deemed slightly beyond the pale at the time, the lyrics – intoned by Troggs singer Reg Presley with seemingly laconic indifference – add to the mysterious appeal of the song, which more or less instantly became associated with the crazy young things of the teenage revolution.

This song begs to be covered, and many a musician has jumped at the chance, tackling 'Wild Thing' in a variety of ways. Who can forget Ned's Atomic Dustbin, featuring the then-alive-and-screaming actor Oliver Reed, performing it on a late-Eighties episode of the British music-TV show *The Word*? You may recall that the Neds' drummer kept

the beat going with his sticks in the tricky call-and-response section, and the band performed that section while adhering to a regular beat, unlike the original version.

MUSICAL LEGACY

A wholly different approach to the song had come in 1967 when Jimi Hendrix played 'Wild Thing' at that year's Monterey Pop Festival. As he'd done with Cream's 'Sunshine Of Your Love' and Chuck Berry's 'Johnny B Goode', Hendrix stretched 'Wild Thing' out into an epic jam marathon, heading off to deliver spiralling fusillades of notes while his band stuck to the original riff. However, not all versions of the song have been so ambitious. Westlife performed an eye-wateringly weak version of the song on tour; *The Muppet Show* featured a cover sung by drummer Animal on the album *Kermit Unpigged* (yes, really); and even Prince threw in a bit of the song while running through a version of Tommy James & The Shondells' 'Crimson And Clover'. Finally, a 1988 cover by the vociferous American comedian Sam Kinison featured Guns N' Roses guitarist Slash and drummer Steven Adler, Steven Tyler and Joe Perry of Aerosmith, Billy Idol and several other stars of the day. Why, you ask? Perhaps they were paid a lot of money.

GENRES

Rock

RECORDED

1966 in London

PRODUCER

Larry Page

BAND MEMBERS

Reg Presley, Chris Britton, Pete Staples, Ronnie Bond

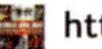
http://flametr.com/wild-thing-troggs

U2

SUNDAY BLOODY SUNDAY

The release of 'Sunday Bloody Sunday' in February 1983 established Irish rock band U2 as protest singers. Troubled by Ireland's bloody history, fuelled by religious convictions and ready to take on the world, the Dublin foursome offered up a very real cry of anguish on the subject of the Bloody Sunday massacre in Derry 11 years previously. Guitarist Dave 'The Edge' Evans began the song with a martial, descending riff that prefaced tribal drums and a raw bass-line, while singer Bono threw everything that his as-yet inexperienced vocal chords had at the song. Listen to the song again now and you'll realize just how far U2 have come in the intervening 30 years. By the mid-Eighties they had become experimentalists, by the early Nineties the arch jesters of rock, and later still a stadium band that is routinely hailed as the biggest live draw in the world. 'Sunday Bloody Sunday' is often given a softer treatment when played live, which suits it just as well or even better than the original, rocked-up version. After all, it's a sensitive song about an appalling moment in history.

GENRES

Rock, post-punk

RECORDED

1982 in Dublin, Ireland

PRODUCER

Steve Lillywhite

BAND MEMBERS

Paul 'Bono' Hewson, Dave 'The Edge' Evans, Adam Clayton, Larry Mullen, Jr

ON YOUTUBE

VAN HALEN

RUNNIN' WITH THE DEVIL

In April 1978 nobody knew who Van Halen were except the couple of thousand or so rock fans who'd caught them live on the Pasadena and California club circuit. That changed, however, when the group – vocalist Dave Lee Roth, guitarist extraordinaire Eddie Van Halen, bassist Michael Anthony and drummer Alex Van Halen – released their debut album. The first song, 'Runnin' With The Devil' showcased so much about Van Halen: Eddie's lightning-in-a-bottle guitar pyrotechnics, Roth's showmanship and the solidity of the rhythm section. Famously, the song begins with Anthony playing single notes in fourths, practically the least complex bass-line possible. That doesn't make it easy, though; as anyone who has ever tried to stick to a simple groove knows, easy guitar parts are also easy to mess up.

RECORDING AND RELEASE

Laid down in late 1977 at the legendary Sunset Sound Recorders studio in Hollywood, 'Runnin' With The Devil' doesn't stick for long to its simple, bread-and-butter introduction. Eddie Van Halen's guitar parts are economical, for sure, but he executes the riffs with panache, throwing in slides and harmonics. Then there's Dave Lee Roth, whose vocals are a masterpiece of improvisation and exposition – at times it seems as if he's going to shred his larynx completely. The solo runs, when they come, are executed with such extrovert perfection that it's easy to understand why Eddie was hailed more or less immediately as a guitar god. The album sold over 10 million albums in the USA alone, earning Van Halen one of their two diamond discs. That's how much America loved Van Halen and, in fairness, they were one of the era's most dynamic groups.

MUSICAL LEGACY

'Runnin' With The Devil' was a cleverer song than most people think. Eddie, the band's founder and mastermind, must have known that his extravagant guitar style would win him fans among the shredder community, but he also knew that simple, effective songwriting is the way to sell records. Kicking the *Van Halen* album off with the ridiculously uncomplicated 'Runnin' With The Devil', which doesn't approach musical complexity until Eddie's first solo, was a good way of turning heads. Note, too, that 'Runnin' With The Devil' is placed right before Eddie's famous solo composition 'Eruption', on which the world heard his neoclassical fretboard tapping for the first time. As an amusing side note, without 'Runnin' With The Devil', the thrash-metal band Megadeth might never have formed. In 1983, bassist David Ellefson was practising that simple bass-line in his Los Angeles apartment. Awoken by the relentless pulse and resenting it, guitarist Dave Mustaine – who lived in the apartment above Ellefson's – threw a plant pot out of his window onto his noisy neighbour's air-conditioning unit. The two men met, hit it off, and formed the band. If Ellefson had been working on a more complex bass part, perhaps Mustaine wouldn't have been quite so irritated and the plant pot might never have been thrown. True story.

GENRES

Heavy metal, hard rock

RECORDED

1977 in Los Angeles

PRODUCER

Ted Templeman

BAND MEMBERS

Dave Lee Roth, Eddie Van Halen, Michael Anthony, Alex Van Halen

ON YOUTUBE  http://flametr.com/runnin-van-halen

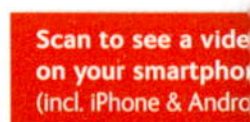

VAN HALEN

AIN'T TALKIN' 'BOUT LOVE

By September 1978, Van Halen had made a significant impact on international rock audiences thanks to a series of singles from the Pasadena quartet's debut album, the latest of which was 'Ain't Talkin' 'Bout Love'. This song, a strange composition in that there is very little to it apart from the world-class riff that begins it, was a major hit, with audiences entranced by its shouted chorus and Eddie Van Halen's unearthly prowess on the guitar.

If anything, the song belongs to bassist Michael Anthony and drummer Alex Van Halen, who keep it anchored firmly to the groove. In fact, it's one of Anthony's finest-ever performances in a career full of highlights.

RECORDING AND RELEASE

What's so special about 'Ain't Talkin' 'Bout Love'? From a guitarist's point of view, pretty much everything that Eddie Van Halen does on the song is extraordinary. When he solos, he throws in harmonics, divebombs and other musical flourishes that were quite simply unheard of at that point in heavy-rock history. In his rhythm playing, Eddie emulated Jimi Hendrix in that his riff work bled into his leads from time to time; at points there is no distinguishing between what he is doing, as all of it is so expressive. Nowhere is this better demonstrated than in 'Ain't Talkin' 'Bout Love''s core riff, an alternate-picked ascending sequence of notes that resolves to an electronically treated peak. The same riff is repeated in the song's mid-section when Eddie plays it softly with a clean guitar tone. It's really quite astounding.

MUSICAL LEGACY

One of the most significant parts of 'Ain't Talkin' 'Bout Love''s story is that it was among the first rock riffs to be sampled in large quantities by hip-hop and electronica artists. Back in the early 1980s, when sampling was first coming into play, the technology was primitive and producers had no way of isolating individual tracks for sampling. In this sense 'Ain't Talkin' 'Bout Love' was a godsend, because Eddie Van Halen had recorded the desired riff at the front of the song, unaccompanied by any other instruments, allowing musicians such as Tone Loc and 2 Live Crew, both rap outfits, to sample his fleet-fingered skills. This was taken to its logical conclusion in 1997 when a British dance act called Apollo 440 made an entire song called 'Ain't Talkin' 'Bout Dub' from the riff (although, of course, by that time sampling was big business and Eddie was paid his dues). Elsewhere, straight covers of the song were performed by Velvet Revolver on the occasion of Van Halen's induction into the Rock And Roll Hall Of Fame in 2007, with Slash making light work of the famous riff, as you would expect. Pearl Jam have had a go at the song too. Finally, Green Day frontman Billie Joe Armstrong occasionally whips out the 'Ain't Talkin' 'Bout Love' riff at live shows. It's just one of *those* riffs – every guitarist wants to learn how to play it, and once it's been learned, it just has to be played.

GENRES

Heavy metal, hard rock

RECORDED

1977 in Los Angeles

PRODUCER

Ted Templeman

BAND MEMBERS

Dave Lee Roth, Eddie Van Halen, Michael Anthony, Alex Van Halen

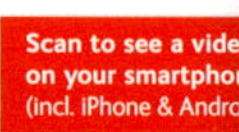

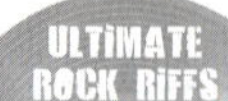

VAN HALEN

PANAMA

The reign of Van Halen continued into the mid-Eighties with this tremendous radio hit about a car that singer Dave Lee Roth had seen in a race called the Panama Express. At this stage in the band's career, guitarist and bandleader Eddie Van Halen was striking gold with every song he wrote. The riff that opens the song is a delayed figure of sheer beauty, as is the entire midsection, over which Eddie solos with his usual inventive brilliance and melodic awareness. Listen out for the sound of Eddie's Lamborghini, revving its engine halfway through the song; the car (an Eighties icon if ever there was one) was reversed into the studio and microphones placed near its exhaust. Let's hope they opened the windows in the control room for a bit afterwards. After another few years in the limelight, in which songs such as 'Jump' kept Van Halen's stock high, fashions changed and personnel shuffles hindered the band's progress. Make no mistake, though, at the time of 'Panama''s release, the group were on top of the world.

GENRES

Hard rock, heavy metal

RECORDED

1983 in Los Angeles

PRODUCER

Ted Templeman

BAND MEMBERS

Dave Lee Roth, Eddie Van Halen, Michael Anthony, Alex Van Halen

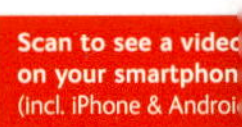

VELVET REVOLVER

SLITHER

Get a pistol and something soft and think of a name for them. Velvet Gun? Revolver N' Roses? Little wonder that when ex-Guns N' Roses members Slash, Matt Sorum and Duff McKagan formed a new group with ex-Stone Temple Pilots singer Scott Weiland and released a debut single in May 2004, the name they chose was a nod to their old band. 'Slither', an excellent moshpit anthem, which builds to an appropriately slippery, Zeppelin-style riff, introduced Velvet Revolver to the world with immense panache and remains their best-known song. Note the long, ominous intro executed by Slash and fellow guitarist Dave Kushner before the main riff breaks out, in which the group are seen prowling the stage in a sleazy nightclub of some description. If dirty rock music is what you're after, look no further, although Velvet Revolver's career has been punctuated with the occasional hiatus. No one, least of all the band members, seems to know whether Velvet Revolver are active or not at the time of writing. Still, 'Slither' would make an appropriate kiss-off for the band if they were no longer in business.

GENRES

Hard rock, heavy metal

RECORDED

2003 in Los Angeles

PRODUCER

Josh Abraham

BAND MEMBERS

Scott Weiland, Saul 'Slash' Hudson, Dave Kushner, Duff McKagan, Matt Sorum

THE WHITE STRIPES

SEVEN NATION ARMY

In March 2003 The White Stripes, a guitarist and drummer who had once been a couple but are now on strictly platonic terms, released their most successful single. 'Seven Nation Army' rested on a guitar riff dropped down a couple of octaves to resemble a bass, courtesy of frontman Jack White and his plastic Airline guitar. That riff continued in a trance-like manner throughout the song, devolving to a bass-only line in the verse and adding shrieked blues guitars for the choruses. It was an instant classic and will be one of the Noughties' most-played songs. The White Stripes themselves never outdid it, calling it a day in 2011 to focus on other projects. A multitude of other groups have covered 'Seven Nation Army', including Metallica, who played a snatch of it at an MTV Awards show, and Audioslave (the supergroup formed by Soundgarden singer Chris Cornell and three members of Rage Against The Machine) played it live. In both cases Jack White's treated guitar line was played on a bass. Hey, if it sounds like a bass guitar, why not play it on one?

GENRES

Alternative rock, garage rock revival

RECORDED

2002 in London

PRODUCER

Jack White

BAND MEMBERS

Jack White, Meg White

http://flametr.com/seven-nation

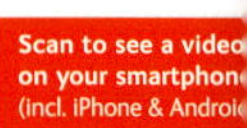

THE WHO

PINBALL WIZARD

The Who's concept album *Tommy* was a radical piece of work, covering a multitude of themes. The main character, the boy of the title, was said to be deaf, dumb and blind, but excelled at playing pinball ('he plays by sense of smell'). In March 1969 'Pinball Wizard' was released as a single, and what a single it was for riff fans. Beginning with that subtle, echoed buildup, the stabbing guitars and then the superb, ethereal chord sequence that leads into the vocal, it is one of the Sixties' defining compositions. Writer Pete Townshend made the most of his band's dynamics, allowing bassist John Entwistle space to move, and focusing on fast-strummed chords rather than solos. Six years after its release, 'Pinball Wizard' was performed by Elton John at a piano in Ken Russell's film adaptation of *Tommy*, with the renowned ivories-tinkler using his own band for the backing track. It's probably the best cover version of the song yet attempted, although amusing covers by McFly and the Flaming Lips have some merit.

GENRES

Rock, hard rock, art rock

RECORDED

1969 in London

PRODUCER

Kit Lambert

BAND MEMBERS

Roger Daltrey, Pete Townshend, John Entwistle, Keith Moon

http://flametr.com/pinball-wizard

THE WHO

I'M FREE

When The Who were in a mellow mood they could write songs of almost psychedelic laid-backness. Much of their July 1969 single 'I'm Free' was exactly that – a crooned paean to taking it easy ('And freedom tastes of reality …'). The riff that begins the song and pushes it along is a slick bit of songwriting, and will test any budding guitarist's barre chord skills. Its lyrics concern the moment when Tommy, the deaf, dumb and blind pinball wizard, regains his senses and celebrates, with the song's place in the concept album whence it came denoted by the snatch of 'Pinball Wizard''s opening riff at its end. 'I'm Free' was released in the UK with the amazing 'Tommy Can You Hear Me?' as its B-side. It has been covered by a couple of bands, notably the Smithereens, and – rather curiously – it was chosen by Saab to soundtrack one of their advertising campaigns. How exactly the concept of freedom is encapsulated by sitting inside a metal box in a traffic jam is not immediately clear to us, but hey, it's a free world.

GENRES

Rock

RECORDED

1968–69 in London

PRODUCER

Kit Lambert

BAND MEMBERS

Roger Daltrey, Pete Townshend, John Entwistle, Keith Moon

ON YOUTUBE  http://flametr.com/im-free-who

THE EDGAR WINTER GROUP

FRANKENSTEIN

Ah, progressive rock. The genre that means you never have to say you're sorry, or more specifically, where you never have to tell the studio engineer to stop the tape. In January 1973, Edgar Winter, the experimental multi-instrumentalist, was at his most ambitious. On the album *They Only Come Out At Night* (which we love, but heavens above, that cover was surely a misjudgment) he composed the suitably monstrous 'Frankenstein', a lengthy song that largely featured then-new synthesizer technology. He didn't forget to throw in some riffs for the rockers, though, notably the staccato figure that begins the song.

RECORDING AND RELEASE

As with so many major hits in the wacky world of pop music, 'Frankenstein' was conceived as a bit of a joke and barely intended to be taken seriously. No doubt Winter, who had performed a version of the song with his brother Johnny as early as 1970, thought that the synth noodling which was laden all over the song like a bag of snakes would doom it to be a novelty song in the public eye. Nothing could have been further from the truth.

When the public heard 'Frankenstein', they inundated radio programmers and DJs with requests for the song. In the studio, it had suffered a difficult birth, rather like the horror-movie monster of the same name. Having been recorded as a song of several minutes' duration, Edgar and the band had to physically cut the tape into pieces with a razor blade to assemble the final edit. That was how everybody did it before digital editing, but then again few songs were as long or as complex as 'Frankenstein', which even boasted a double drum solo.

MUSICAL LEGACY

Bands and musicians who have appreciated 'Frankenstein' enough to attempt a cover version of the song come from all corners of the musical arena. It's jazz-based, especially in the synth sections, which explains why sometime Miles Davis bassist Marcus Miller had a go at it. But that doesn't explain why New Jersey thrash-metal band Overkill decided to reanimate the monster. Then again, perhaps the significance of 'Frankenstein' is not primarily that other groups have covered it. The truth is that when Edgar Winter played the song live, he established a grim precedent by becoming the first ever keyboard player to strap on his instrument and walk on stage to play it in the same position as a guitar. Nowadays, of course, the 'keytar' or portable keyboard unit with a 'neck' is a common sight, especially among progressive metal bands, but back then the concept of taking your synth off its glorified ironing-board, nailing a couple of screws to it and hanging it around your neck was practically enough to get you arrested. A nation of prog fans, specifically those who play keyboards, owe Edgar an eternal debt as a result. The album cover is still awful, though.

GENRES

Instrumental rock

RECORDED

1972 in New York

PRODUCER

Rick Derringer

BAND MEMBERS

Edgar Winter, Dan Hartman, Randy Jo Hobbs, Johnny Badanjek

http://flametr.com/frankenstein-winter

Scan to see a video on your smartphone (incl. iPhone & Android

NEIL YOUNG & CRAZY HORSE

HEY HEY, MY MY (INTO THE BLACK)

By August 1979 and at the grand old age of 34, Canadian singer-songwriter Neil Young was beginning to feel a bit long in the tooth. Punk had happened, causing him to wonder whether his music still had a place in the modern world. Accordingly, his 1979 album *Live Rust* featured two similarly titled songs, 'My My, Hey Hey (Out Of The Blue)' and 'Hey Hey, My My (Into The Black)'. The latter was based on a full-fat, distorted guitar riff that you could easily mistake for a grunge pattern from the early 1990s if it weren't for Young's instantly identifiable vocal line on top of it. The rust metaphor was Young's way of analysing his own compositional skills. Could he get away with releasing more of the same old music (in other words, 'rusting'), or should he explore new territory? With the assistance of punk pioneers Devo, with whom he occasionally collaborated, he did both, and spent some years working in different musical arenas until he returned to his old style in his later career.

GENRES

Hard rock, proto-grunge

RECORDED

1978 in San Francisco

PRODUCER

Neil Young

BAND MEMBERS

Neil Young, Frank Sampedro, Billy Talbot, Ralph Molina

http://flametr.com/hey-hey

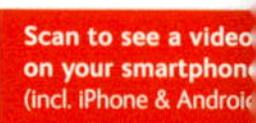

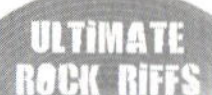

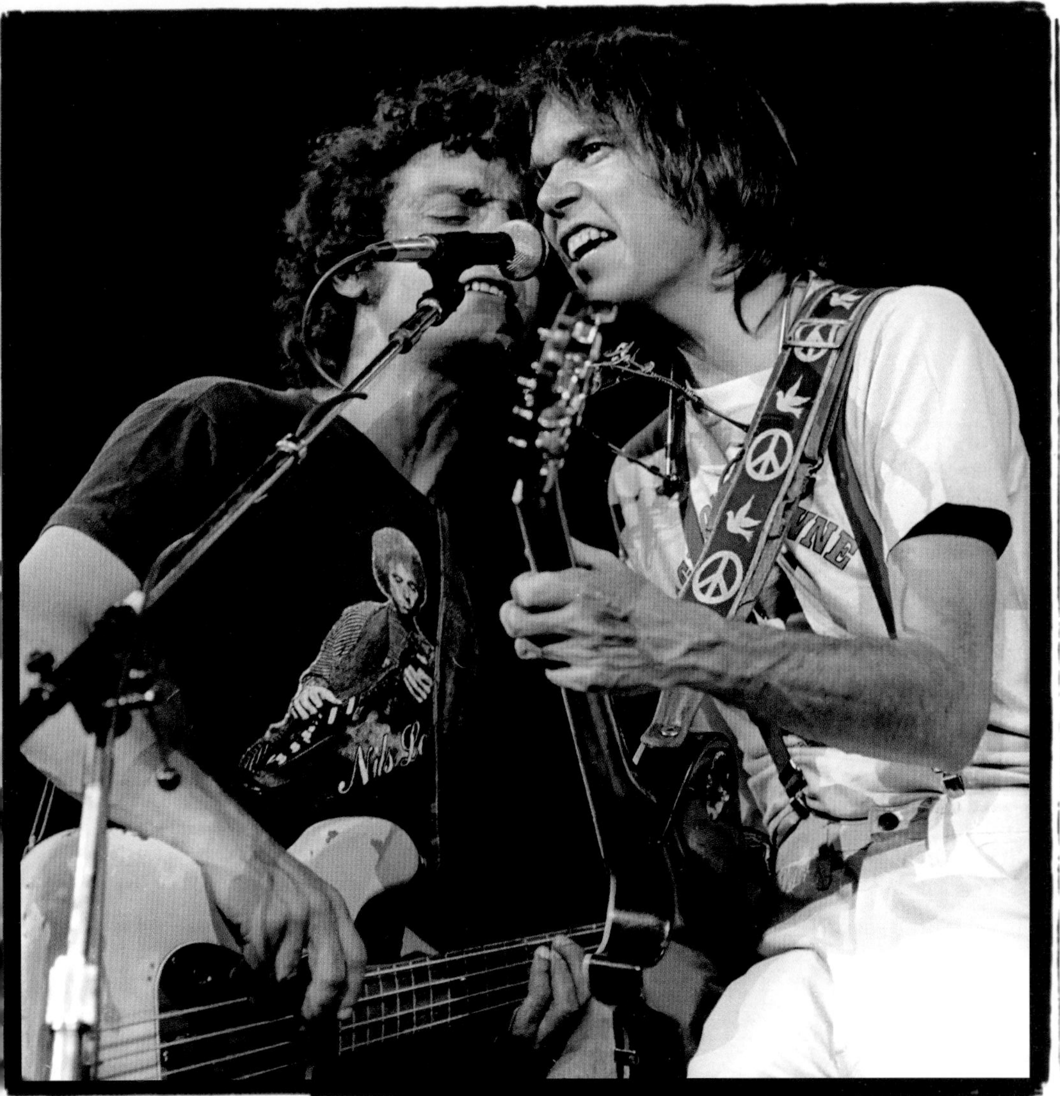

ZZ TOP

GIMME ALL YOUR LOVIN'

Although Texan rock trio ZZ Top had been a successful recording and touring act for over a decade by March 1983, it was in that month that they first tasted truly international success, thanks to the single 'Gimme All Your Lovin''. The secret lay in Billy Gibbons's guitar sound, a deep, Sabbathy rock/metal hybrid that perfectly complemented the solid, unintrusive bass and drums. The hooky chorus line was a winner too, and the trio's image of fast car plus beards (except drummer Frank Beard, perhaps the most over-quoted instance of irony ever) pulled in audiences by the million. Who were these people, crowds asked, before playing air guitar to this song and the singles that followed, none of which deviated radically from the hard-rock template. Before this key period in ZZ Top's history, the group didn't sound anything like this. They had focused more on a roots sound, eschewing the polished radio rock that eventually made them rich. Interesting fact, Gillette Razors offered Gibbons and bassist Dusty Hill a million dollars each to shave off their beards. They declined, because they didn't need the money.

GENRES

Hard rock

RECORDED

1982 in Memphis

PRODUCER

Bill Ham

BAND MEMBERS

Billy Gibbons, Dusty Hill, Frank Beard

ON YOUTUBE  http://flametr.com/gimme-lovin

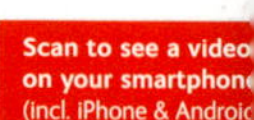

FURTHER READING

Bogdanov, V. (ed.), et al, *All Music Guide to Rock*, Backbeat, London, 2002

Buskin, R., *Inside Tracks: A First-Hand History of Popular Music from the World's Greatest Record Producers and Engineers*, Avon, New York, 1999

Canter, M., *Reckless Road: Guns N' Roses and the Making of Appetite For Destruction*, Future Publishing, London, 2012

Capone, P., *100 Killer Riffs & Fills for Rock Guitar*, Chartwell Books, Minneapolis, 2012

Christie, I., *Everybody Wants Some: The Van Halen Saga*, John Wiley & Sons, Hoboken, 2008

Classic Rock Riffs: Over 40 Essential Classics, Hal Leonard Publishing, Milwaukee, 2012

Cutchin, R. (ed.), *The Illustrated Encyclopedia of Guitar Heroes*, Flame Tree Publishing, London, 2008

Dimery, R. (ed.), *1001 Albums You Must Hear Before You Die*, Cassell Illustrated, London, 2008

Dimery, R. (ed.), *1001 Songs You Must Hear Before You Die*, Cassell Illustrated, London, 2010

Draper, J., *Led Zeppelin Revealed*, Flame Tree Publishing, London, 2008

Draper, J., *The Rolling Stones Revealed*, Flame Tree Publishing, London, 2007

Du Noyer, P. (ed.), *The Illustrated Encyclopedia of Music*, Flame Tree Publishing, London, 2003

Fielder, H., *The Beatles Revealed*, Flame Tree Publishing, London, 2010

George-Warren, H. et al, *The Rolling Stone Encyclopedia of Rock & Roll*, Fireside, New York, 2001

Graff, G. and Durchholz, D., *MusicHound Rock: The Essential Album Guide*, Omnibus Press, London, 1998

Harrison, H., *Kurt Cobain, Beyond Nirvana: The Legacy of Kurt Cobain*, The Archives Press, 1994

Heatley, M. (ed.), *Top 100 Rock: Bands, Acts, Artists*, Flame Tree Publishing, London, 2010

Heatley, M. and Brown, A., *How To Play Rock: Riffs, Rhythm & Lead*, Flame Tree Publishing, London, 2008

Hopkins, J., *The Jimi Hendrix Experience*, Arcade Publishing, New York, 1996

Ingham, C., *The Book of Metal*, Carlton Books, London, 2002

Iommi, T., *Iron Man: My Journey Through Heaven and Hell with Black Sabbath*, Simon & Schuster Ltd, London, 2011

Jeffries, N. (ed.), *The "Kerrang!" Direktory of Heavy Metal: The Indispensable Guide to Rock Warriors and Headbangin' Heroes*, Virgin Books, London, 1993

Kent, M., *The Who Revealed*, Flame Tree Publishing, London, 2010

Kozinn, A., *The Beatles*, Phaidon, London, 1995

Larkin, C., *Encyclopedia of Popular Music*, Virgin Publishing, London, 2002

Larkin, C., *The Guinness Who's Who of Sixties Music*, Guinness Publishing, London, 1992

Larkin, C., *The Virgin Encyclopedia of Heavy Rock*, Virgin Books, London, 1999

Larkin, C., *The Virgin Illustrated Encyclopedia of Rock*, Virgin Books, London, 1999

Logan, N. and Woffinden, B. (eds.), *The Illustrated New Musical Express Encyclopedia of Rock*, Hamlyn, London, 1976

McIver, J., *The Bloody Reign of Slayer*, Omnibus Press, London, 2008

McIver, J., *The 100 Greatest Metal Guitarists*, Jawbone, London, 2007

The Riffology: Learn To Play 140 Classic Guitar Riffs, Music Sales Own, 2010

Riffs and Rhythms Rock Anthems, Wise Publications, London, 2007

Rooksby, R., *Riffs: How To Create and Play Great Guitar Riffs*, Backbeat Books, London, 2002

Smith, J., *Off the Record: An Oral History of Popular Music*, Grand Central Publishing, New York, 1989

Spicer, A., *The Rough Guide to Rock (100 Essential CDs)*, Rough Guides, London, 1999

Strong, M.C., *The Great Rock Discography*, Canongate Publications, Edinburgh, 2002

Sutcliffe, P., *AC/DC: The Ultimate Illustrated History*, Voyageur Press Inc, 2010

Troup, S., *The Rifftionary: 132 of the World's Most Famous Guitar Riffs*, Faber Music, London, 2004

Whitburn, J., *Billboard Top 1000 Singles 1955–2000*, Hal Leonard Publishing, Milwaukee, 2001

ACKNOWLEDGEMENTS

AUTHOR BIOGRAPHIES

Robb Flynn (Foreword)

Robb Flynn is the founder, frontman and guitarist of Bay Area-based metal band Machine Head. The winners of many awards for their music, three million records sold, and a 2008 Grammy nomination, Machine Head have toured the world since 1994 and have played alongside the planet's biggest bands. As a riff writer, Flynn has anchored Machine Head with his incisive, uncompromising approach to his craft, delivering the riffage these days via his signature Epiphone 'Love Death' Flying V. Machine Head's latest album, *Unto The Locust*, was hailed on its release in 2011 as the metal album of the year in many publications.

Joel McIver (Author)

Joel McIver is the author of 20 books on music: another 30 exist in translation. His best-known book is 2004's *Justice For All: The Truth About Metallica*, which has sold close to 50,000 copies in several languages. He regularly appears on radio and TV and was labelled 'the top rock scribe writing today' in a 2009 anthology of music writing, but don't worry, he's really an OK guy. You can reach him via his website: www.joelmciver.co.uk.

Joel would like to dedicate this book to the splendid racket made by the following musicians: Matt Bellamy, Chuck Berry, Ritchie Blackmore, David Bowie, Eric Clapton, Ray Davies, Steve Harris, James Hetfield, Tony Iommi, Kerry King, Geddy Lee, Lemmy, Tom Morello, Dave Mustaine, Jimmy Page, Joe Perry, Nikki Sixx, Slash, Pete Townshend, Eddie Van Halen, Angus Young, Neil Young. RIP 'Dimebag' Darrell Abbott, Kurt Cobain, Jimi Hendrix, John Lennon, Phil Lynott and Randy Rhoads. You made the world a better (and much louder) place.

PICTURE CREDITS

All images courtesy of **Getty Images** and the following collections: ABC: 95; Archive Photos: 55, 219, 303; FilmMagic: 41, 43, 157, 299; Ron Galella Collection: 147; Getty Images Entertainment: 87, 227, 233; Hulton Archive: 35, 81, 187, 201, 209, 235, 279, Terry O'Neill: 73, 241; Michael Ochs Archives: 27, 29, 33, 53, 77, 79, 93, 101, 103, 113, 115, 117, 119, 125, 137, 141, 143, 145, 149, 165, 167, 183, 213, 267, 269, 271; Popperfoto: 45, 159; Premium Archive: 51, 57, 131, 253; Redferns: 37, 39, 47, 49, 59, 61, 65, 67, 69, 75, 83, 85, 91, 97, 99, 105, 109, 121, 127, 129, 133, 135, 139, 151, 153, 155, 161, 163, 171, 173, 177, 181, 195, 197, 199, 203, 205, 207, 211, 215, 217, 225, 237, 239, 243, 247, 249, 251, 255, 257, 259, 261, 263, 265, 273, 277, 281, 283, 285, 287, 289, 293, 295, 297, 301, 307, 309, 311, 313; Sony Music Archive: 231; Time & Life Pictures: 189, 245; WireImage: 31, 63, 71, 89, 107, 111, 123, 169, 175, 179, 185, 191, 193, 221, 223, 229, 275, 291, 305.

INDEX

Page references in **bold** refer to main articles, those in *italics* to illustrations of artists, bands or band members. Hyphenated page references take no account of intervening illustrations. Album titles are in *italics* and song titles are in inverted commas.